The Crusades

PETER MANTIN
AND RICHARD PULLEY

Hodder & Stoughton
LONDON SYDNEY AUCKLAND

ACKNOWLEDGEMENTS

The Publishers would like to thank the following for permission to reproduce material in this volume:

Cambridge University Press for extracts from *The Cambridge History of Islam*, P. M. Holt (ed.), 1970 and *History of the Crusades*, S. Runciman, 1951; John Murray (Publishers) Ltd. for the extract from *Approaches to Islam*, Richard Tames, 1982; Macmillan Education Ltd for extract from *What Were the Crusades?*, J. Riley-Smith; Oxford University Press for the extract from *Islam from the Prophet Muhammad to the Capture of Constantinople*, Bernard Lewis (ed.), 1984; Weidenfeld & Nicolson Ltd for the extracts from *Chronicles of the Crusades*, E. Hallam (ed.), 1989.

The Publishers would also like to thank the following for permission to reproduce copyright illustrations in this volume:

La Cantiga 181 del Manuscrito "Cantigas de Santa Maria", La Biblioteca de El Escorial – cover.
Ms Egerton 1500 f. 45v, The British Library p. 5 left.
Ms 4276 f. 6, La Bibliothèque Nationale p. 5 right.
The Kobal Collection p. 6.
Royal Ms 2A. XXII f. 220, The British Library p. 7 top left.
Add Ms 42130 f. 82, The British Library p. 7 lower.
Wales Tourist Board p. 8.
A.F. Kersting p.10.
Cotton Nero C IV f. 39, The British Library p. 11.
Ms 9087 f. 85v, La Bibliothèque Nationale/Edimedia p. 12.
Sonia Halliday Photo Library p. 13.
Ms Roy 16 G VI f. 436 v, The British Library p. 14.
Codex 120 II f. 143r, Burgerbibliothek Bern, p. 15 top right.
The Hulton-Deutsch Collection Ltd p. 15 lower right.
Add Ms 22557 f. 9v, The British Library p. 16.
Add Ms 27376 f. 45, The British Library p. 17.
The Hulton-Deutsch Collection Ltd p. 18.
Fr. 5594 f. 21, La Bibliothèque Nationale p. 19 left.
Sonia Halliday Photo Library p. 19 right.
Ms Fr 9084, f. 20 v La Bibliothèque Nationale p. 22 left.

The Hulton-Deutsch Collection Ltd p. 22 right.
Codex Gigas, A148 Kungliga Biblioteket p. 24 right.
Reproduced by permission of the Master & Fellows of Corpus Christi College, Cambridge, Ms 16 f. 54v p. 24 lower.
Ms Cotton Nero D II f. 183v, The British Library p. 25.
Codex 2533 f. 7 v, Osterreichisches Nationalbibliothek p. 26.
Ms Fr. 352 f. 62, La Bibliothèque Nationale p. 27.
Swanston Graphics, Derby p. 28–29.
Ms Add 27376 f. 4v, The British Library p. 30.
Ms Add 15268 f. 101v, The British Library p. 33.
Roy 16 GVI, f. 350, The British Library p. 34.
Roger Hall/Ladybird Books p. 34.
The Kobal Collection p. 35 top left.
Roy 14 C VII f. 9, The British Library p. 35 lower left.
Codex 120 III f. 129r, Burgerbibliothek Bern p. 35 right.
The British Museum p. 36 top.
The British Library/Bridgeman Art Library p. 36 lower.
Fr 224495, f. 215 v, La Bibliothèque Nationale p. 37.
Fr 2630, f. 22v, La Bibliothèque Nationale p. 42 left.
Or Ms 20 f. 124v, Edinburgh University Library p. 42 right.
By Permission of the Masters & Fellows of Corpus Christi College, Cambridge, Ms 16, f. 166v p. 43 top.
Photo Hirmer Verlag p. 44.
English Heritage p. 48.
Alan Sorrel/CADW, Welsh Historic Monuments, Crown Copyright p. 49 top left.
Aerofilms p. 49 bottom left.
Sonia Halliday Photo Library p. 51 right.
Ms Fr 9081 f. 99v, La Bibliothèque Nationale p. 52.
Ms Fr 352 f. 49 v, La Bibliothèque Nationale p. 53.
Service Photographique de la Réunion des Musées de Paris p. 54.
© Syndication International Ltd. p. 55.

Every effort has been made to trace and acknowledge ownership of copyright. The Publishers will be glad to make suitable arrangements with any copyright holders whom it has not been possible to contact.

Dedication – To Roger, Chris and Rosalind.

Illustrations by Joseph McEwan

British Library Cataloguing in Publication Data

Mantin, Peter
  Crusades. – (Past Historic Series)
  I. Title II. Pulley, Richard III. Series
  909.07

  ISBN 0–340–56854–2

First published 1993

Impression number 10 9 8 7 6 5 4 3 2 1
Year   1998 1997 1996 1995 1994 1993

© 1993 Peter Mantin and Richard Pulley

Typeset by Litho Link Ltd, Welshpool, Powys, Wales
Printed in Hong Kong for the educational publishing division of Hodder & Stoughton Ltd, Mill Road, Dunton Green, Sevenoaks, Kent by Colorcraft Ltd

CONTENTS

1 Thinking About the Crusades   4
2 Europe in the Middle Ages   8
3 Christianity in Europe   10
4 Jerusalem   12
5 Who Went Crusading?   14
6 Travelling East   18
7 Islam in the 11th Century   20
8 The First Crusade   22
9 Images of the East   24
10 The Siege of Jerusalem   26
11 Living in Palestine   28
12 Crusades of the 12th Century   32
13 Richard I   34
14 Saladin   36
15 Crusades of the 13th Century   38
16 Crusades in Europe   40
17 Siege Warfare   42
18 Templars and Hospitallers   44
19 Effects of the Crusades   46
20 Timeline   52
21 Change and Continuity   54
Glossary   56
Index   57

Highlighted words are explained in the glossary on page 56.

1000	1050	1100	1150	1200	1250	1300

We watch the news on television and what do we see? Arguments. People don't seem to be able to agree about very much; should we build a road here or there? Should we raise taxes or not? Ought we to go to war?

Of course, there is nothing wrong with arguing about things. After all, the outcome is often very important – and disagreements do not stop people being friends. So it is not surprising that historians debate, or argue about, what happened in the past.

The historians' job is to put forward their own *ideas* about the past. These must be based on all the evidence that they can find. Almost always someone, somewhere, will disagree with these ideas, so a debate will start and new ideas will develop. Why is this?

Well, the world changes and people's interests and ways of looking at things change. In the rest of this chapter there are a few examples of things that you should think about as you study this topic.

There are different ways of understanding what happened in the past. We need to think about how these different points of view have come about. Then we can begin to make up our own minds.

What Were the Crusades?

For most people 'the crusades' is the name given to events in the Middle Ages. Large armies of Christian soldiers and ordinary people travelled from Western Europe to the Middle East. They were trying to take control of places linked with the life of Jesus Christ, especially the city of Jerusalem.

The trouble was that these areas were controlled by Turks and Arabs who were Muslims . They would not let foreign armies take their land without a fight; Jerusalem was just as holy to them as it was to Christians.

A Western Europe and the Middle East at the time of the crusades.

The First Crusade set out in 1096 and captured Jerusalem. There then followed at least seven other crusades to the East up to 1271.

Such a brief story covers up a lot of problems that might cause historians to argue with each other. First of all, 'crusade' is a Western European idea. The word 'crusade' wasn't even used at the time; it was only with the Third 'Crusade' of 1188 that a word anything like 'crusade' was made to describe what was happening. It was only in the 16th century that the word was used in English.

To the people of the Middle East, the crusades just looked like a whole series of invasions. Some big, some small, some very warlike, others peaceful. Few of them got anywhere near Jerusalem. They seemed to many of the Muslims, Jews and Christians who lived in the Middle East like an attempt to gain land. After all, Christians had been going to visit Jerusalem ever since the 4th century. What was different in the 11th century was the military organisation and huge numbers of people involved.

So how religious were the crusades? Is 'crusade' a good word to describe these events? What do historians today think about the crusades? What questions do you have about the crusades? Talk about these questions as you work through this material.

C Getting ready to go East. Supplies being organised. The picture was made in the 14th century.

B Peter the Hermit leading pilgrims to the East in 1096. The picture was made in the 14th century.

1 a) Look at source B. What kind of people does it show going on a crusade?
   b) Source B shows a number of soldiers. Does this prove that *all* crusades were warlike? Explain your answer carefully.
   c) 'Source C proves that the crusades were always well supplied.' Is this statement true or false? Explain your answer carefully.

2 a) Using both sources B and C write a paragraph saying what you can work out from these pictures.
   b) How could we check to find out if they were accurate sources of evidence?

3 a) If a historian writes a book about the crusades *without* using every single source of evidence about them does this mean that the book is no good? Give reasons to explain your answer.
   b) Give some reasons why the word 'crusade' might not be the right word to describe the journeys to the Middle East.

HISTORIANS AND THE CRUSADES

What have historians written about the crusades? Here we look at the ideas of a number of people. Notice how ideas about the past change. Try to think about why this happens.

Read the sources on this page very carefully and look at the pictures before you answer any of the questions.

Over the years, historians have taken different views about the crusades. Sources A–D show four different attitudes. Each has been simplified from the original.

A Thomas Fuller in the 17th century wrote that the only person who gained from the crusades was the Pope . From a book called *The Holy War* written in 1639.

All other princes of Europe, find themselves losers. The Pope, for his own benefit, made all Jerusalem, a place for skulls, and all the Holy Land, a field of blood.

B Voltaire, an 18th-century French writer, asked why the princes of Europe could claim lands which had not been theirs in the first place.

C William Robertson, an 18th-century Scottish historian, saw the crusades as a mistake. However, he believed that the contact with the Middle East did lead to greater wealth and was a good influence on Europe.

D The view of English historian Edward Gibbon in the 18th century:

The crusades brought about great and rapid progress. Some have praised the influence of those holy wars, which appear to me to have stopped rather than advanced Europe.

The millions who were buried in the East would have been better used in the improvement of their own country.

You might have found this a bit difficult. What Gibbon says is: millions of people were killed in the East when they could have been working to make Europe richer and more civilised.

E Amin Maalouf, an Arab writer, wrote in *The Crusades Through Arab Eyes* (1983) that:

It looked as if the Arab world had won a great victory. If the West had tried, through all its invasions, to control Islam , the result was the opposite. The new crusader states of the Middle East only lasted two centuries. The Muslims had gained the upper hand and, before long, they would try to conquer Europe itself. By 1529 they had reached Vienna. However, the Muslims were weakened by the crusades. They have never recovered from the violence which Western European armies did to them during the crusades.

F Saladin and Richard meet: a photograph from a film made about the crusades.

G A crusader praying. This English picture was made in the 13th century.

1. Source H was made almost 200 years after the time it shows. Does this mean that it is of no use to a historian interested in the crusades? Give reasons.

2. What are (a) the similarities and (b) the differences between sources F and H?

3. Saladin did not look like the person shown in source H. Why do you think he has been painted in this ugly way?

4. Read the following sentences and say if you think that they are true or false. Explain your answers carefully.
   a) 'All historians writing after the 16th century thought that the crusades were a "bad thing".' (Mention names, dates and what people say.)
   b) 'Nobody will be able to write a book about the crusades without someone else finding something wrong with it.'
   c) 'Arab historians writing about the crusades will always write about different things from European historians.'

5. Look at source G. How can you tell that this is a Christian knight?

H A picture of Saladin (right) fighting King Richard I of England. They were both important leaders during the 12th century. This picture was made in the 14th century.

Historians need to explain why things happen. First, they must study what people at the time did and thought. This is not easy and is one reason why historians often disagree with each other.

The Feudal System

Looking back to the time of the First Crusade in 1096 it seems to us that Western Europe was entering a period of great wealth and expansion. It lasted for about 200 years and created some of the most impressive buildings and works of art of any period in history. It was also the time of the great crusades to the Middle East. What brought this about?

We (the writers) think that it had a lot to do with the way people and land were organised. All of Western Europe was organised into something called the feudal system. This way of arranging things gave almost everyone some land in return for some duties.

At the top were kings, who benefited most from the system. They were followed by the major landowners who had titles like baron, duke or lord. These people owned huge areas of land given to them by the king and were supposed to help him govern as part of their duties.

Next came smaller landowners, often called knights, although they didn't always have a title. They held land given to them by the king or larger landowners. They, too, had to do duties such as giving the king money when there was a war.

Most of the people of Europe were peasants, which means that they owned little or no land. They worked a lot of the time on farms belonging to richer landowners. There were lots of different peasants, but they all worked very hard and had little freedom.

A Pembroke Castle, Wales. The central keep was built in about 1200. Notice the size and position of the castle.

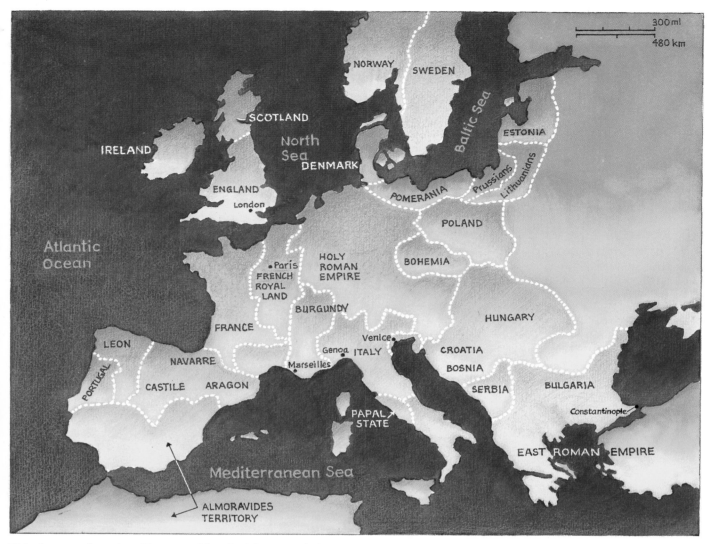

B A map showing Europe, North Africa and the Middle East in 1150.

The feudal system was supposed to unite all the people under the leadership of the king; in fact, it divided them. The peasants tried to stop the knights and other landowners making them work too hard or pay too much tax. The landowners were always trying to get the peasants to work harder for them and pay higher taxes. At the same time, they wanted the king to give them more land.

The king needed the help of the barons in ruling the country. He didn't want to give them too much land in case they became powerful enough to fight him.

This situation caused a lot of hardship and problems. However it also brought about some changes. People were looking for ways to improve their lives. This encouraged the development of new technology, laws, treaties and trade. All these changes helped people to make more money and so parts of Europe became quite rich.

1 a) Using an atlas find the names of *four* countries that were once part of the **East Roman Empire**.
b) Find the names of three countries that were once part of the **Holy Roman Empire**.
c) Using source B name the places a crusader travelling from Paris to Constantinople would have to pass through.

2 Look at source B and a modern atlas showing the same area. How have the borders of countries changed?

3 Explain in your own words: (a) who gained the most from the feudal system; (b) who did not do very well from the feudal system.

4 Are these statements true or false?
a) 'A king was always very powerful in his own country'.
b) 'A lot of people would want to try to get away from the feudal system'. Explain your answers carefully.

3 CHRISTIANITY IN EUROPE

Historians have to explain why people do things. They often discover that there are lots of reasons. As you read this chapter, think about how important the church was in getting people to go on crusades.

The feudal system made the Church and kings rich – but it does not completely explain why the crusades started. The money that they cost could have been spent on building castles or cathedrals at home. So why did people go on crusades?

We would suggest that the power of the Christian Church is very important. Christianity gave people a way of looking at the world. It explained things that they didn't understand or were not sure about. From the 1st century AD the power of the Christian Church had grown. By 1096 no king in Europe could ignore its wishes.

A Salisbury Cathedral, built between 1220 and 1258. This building is an English version of the cathedrals that were being built in France. The tower and spire were built in the 14th century.

Power and Problems

The Church was very well organised and had an international network of men and women to make sure it ran smoothly. At its head was the Pope who lived in Rome. What he said was usually obeyed. The Christian Church was getting bigger – but it was divided. Some Christians had different ideas about how to understand Jesus's teaching. The Pope usually saw these people as very dangerous and tried to stop them spreading their ideas. But most of all the Christian Church feared those with a totally different religion.

During the Middle Ages Christianity was growing stronger because its ideas inspired new ways of living and praying. People believed in it so much that they were willing to do almost anything to show their faith . The Church also owned much land and collected lots of money through taxes. As a result, it was very rich.

The Local Church

The largest building in a medieval village or town was often the church. Almost everybody went to a service there at least once a week. The parish priest led these services. Sometimes he was the only person in the village who could read. He gave the peasants news about what was happening in the world.

The church wasn't just used for services. Feasts were sometimes held in church on holy days. That is where we get the word 'holiday' from. Sometimes the church was used as a bank, where people could leave their money. Old pictures show archery practice taking place in churchyards – so that people could be ready for war.

The local church was a meeting place as well as a place of worship. The church grounds sometimes had markets and Punch and Judy shows in them. It could also be a place of sanctuary. This means that criminals could hide in the safety of the church. Finally, the Church had its own courts. The courts could punish priests as well as ordinary people who had broken church laws.

People in the Middle Ages believed that even if life was very difficult for you on earth, you could look forward to going to heaven when you died. There you would enjoy everlasting happiness. However, people who had done evil deeds would go to hell and be made to suffer for ever.

God would decide who went to heaven or hell at the Last Judgement. This would take place at the end of the world. He would decide by weighing the good deeds against the bad from the souls of the dead.

B This decorated book cover from the 12th century gives a view into hell. The door is being locked by an angel.

1 Write down what you can about each of the following:
   a) the Pope;
   b) the Christian Church in Europe;
   c) the village church.
2 Read these sentences and say if you think that they are true or false. Explain your answer carefully.
   a) 'Source A proves that the Church was very wealthy'.
   b) 'The Church could force everyone to go on a crusade'.
   c) 'Everyone in the world was a Christian in the Middle Ages.'
3 a) What does source B show?
   b) What can you work out from it about people's ideas?

JERUSALEM

A A medieval picture of Jerusalem, painted in 1455.

The main target for many people taking part in the First Crusade was Jerusalem. It was such an important place for Christians in the Middle Ages that they often placed it at the centre of their maps of the world.

They often drew Jerusalem as if it were circular because it was thought that the circle was a perfect shape.

What was so special about Jerusalem? What was so important about this place that Christians, Muslims and Jews were prepared to die trying to capture it?

To Christians, Jerusalem was the place where Christ had been buried and had risen again. It was the city of the prophets and kings of Israel. Jesus had died in Jerusalem. Christians believed that they could walk along the same streets that Christ had walked, and visit some of the places he

had stayed at. Jerusalem was the city of God, so it was important that it did not fall into the hands of 'unbelievers'.

But in the early 11th century Jerusalem was controlled by Muslims and not by Christians. The Islamic faith had begun in Arabia. The word of God was announced by the Prophet Muhammad, who died in 632. Within a few years of his death the Islamic religion had spread throughout Arabia and into the Persian and Byzantine Empires. Iraq, Syria and Persia were conquered. In 711 Islamic armies invaded Spain.

A mighty empire spread across Europe, Africa and Asia; it stretched from the Atlantic Ocean to the borders of China. Jerusalem was only one of many cities which fell to Islam, but it was very special to Muslims.

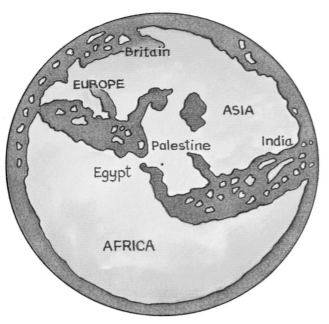

B An 11th-century Arabic map of the world. (The map has been redrawn.)

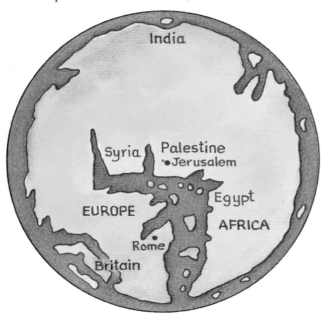

C Medieval Christian map of the world, showing Jerusalem at the centre. (The map has been redrawn.)

D Robert the Monk explained why Jerusalem was so important to Christians and called on crusaders to set it free.

Jerusalem is a land which is fruitful above all others, like a paradise of delights. Christ lived there and made it holy by his suffering. This royal city is now held by its enemies and is enslaved by people who do not know God.

Therefore the city demands to be set free and calls on you to come to its aid. Therefore take this journey for your sins to be forgiven, certain of the glory of the kingdom of heaven.

E The Dome of the Rock, a Muslim holy place in Jerusalem, built around 700.

F A Muslim traveller described a visit to Jerusalem in 1046. He wrote this in his diary.

By 5 March 1046 I was in Jerusalem. The people of Syria called Jerusalem the Holy City. Any Syrian who cannot perform the pilgrimage to Makkah will visit Jerusalem and offer a sacrifice according to custom.

Some years, more than 20,000 people are there. From many regions come Christians and Jews in large numbers to worship at the church and synagogue there.

The great Dome stands on twelve pillars around the Rock. When you look at it from a distance of three miles the Dome appears like the top of a mountain. The roof and ceiling of the building are clothed in carved wood and the pillars are of a style rarely seen elsewhere. Around the Rock they have made a marble balustrade to stop people touching it. The Rock is of a blue coloured stone. No one has ever stepped on it.

In this section we are looking at what maps can tell us about the city of Jerusalem. Today we can take it for granted that a map's main purpose is to help us to find our way somewhere, but can a map be used to tell us other things?

1 Compare sources B and C.
   a) What differences do you notice?
   b) What similarities do you notice?
   c) Suggest reasons for the differences.
2 In what way is source C different from a modern map of the world?
3 Look at sources B and C. Which source was more useful for giving an accurate idea of the world?
4 Which of the sources is the most reliable for finding out about Jerusalem at the time of the First Crusade?

5 WHO WENT CRUSADING?

Historians are interested in what makes people do the things that they do. We call these things motives. In these chapters we are going to look at the motives for going on a crusade.

Thinking about why people went on a crusade helps us to understand who went on them. You can see from the sources you have studied that all sorts of people set off on the dangerous journey east.

But what do we know about the kinds of people who set out for the East? In this chapter are some sources of evidence that help us begin to answer the question.

Study them carefully before answering the questions.

A J Riley-Smith: *What Were the Crusades?* (1977).
In Lincolnshire they were nearly all poor and included a clerk, a smith, a skinner, a potter, a butcher and a vintner; 43 crusaders were to be found in Cornwall, including a tailor, a smith, a shoe maker, 2 chaplains, a merchant, a miller, 2 tanners and 2 women.

B From *The Journey Through Wales* by Gerald of Wales, written soon after 1188.
Some of the worst criminals of the area . . . robbers, highwaymen and murderers, were among the volunteers.

C Louis IX takes a vow in 1244 to lead a crusade and is given a cross. This picture was made about 200 years later.

D From *What Were the Crusades?* by J Riley-Smith (1977).

In the year 1250:
The ship St Victor, bound from France to the East, was carrying 453 crusaders, of whom:
14 were Knights and leaders of the group;
90   retainers ;
7   clerics ;
of the remaining; 342 passengers were commoners and the surnames of several of them suggest merchant origins;
42 were women, 15 of whom were with their husbands. One travelled with her father and two with their brothers.

E From *Alexiad* by Anna Comnena, written in about 1136. She was the daughter of the Byzantine Emperor at the time of the First Crusade. Here, she describes the followers of Peter the Hermit:

There was such universal eagerness and enthusiasm that every highway had some of them; along with soldiers went a large unarmed crowd, carrying palms and crosses on their shoulders, including even women and children who had left their own countries. To look upon them was like seeing rivers flowing together from all sides, and coming against us in full force . . .

G A   manuscript   picture showing Frederick II about to start on a crusade in 1228. The picture was made in 1500.

F Some crusades were not led by kings or princes. According to the *Historia Maiora* by Matthew Paris written in 1251, a 60-year-old Hungarian led a crusade of shepherds who gradually began to follow him:

. . . leaving their flocks and herds . . . without asking their lords or relatives what they wanted . . . Their numbers reached 100,000 or more.

This particular crusade never got further than the South of France but was typical of a number of crusades which were made up of the poor.

H A picture made in the 19th century showing children setting out on the so-called 'Children's Crusade' of 1212. In fact not very many children really went on it and they never reached the Middle East.

---

1 a) Using this chapter, draw up a list of the types of people who went on the crusades.
   b) Look back at pages 12–13 and try to add other types to your list.
   c) For each person, write down at least *one* reason *why* they might be on a crusade.

2 From all the sources in this and the last chapter write down the names of the countries which crusaders came from.

3 The picture sources were made a long time after the events that they show. Does this mean that they are no good as evidence about: (a) the crusades, or (b) armour of the 15-16th centuries? Give reasons for your view.

4 'Most of the people who went crusading were poor'. Is this statement true or false? Explain your answer carefully.

WHY GO ON A CRUSADE?

> In this section we want to begin thinking carefully about the ways sources can be used to answer different kinds of questions.

We have seen the Christian Church was an important influence in people's lives. It encouraged people to go on crusades. But were there other reasons why people might risk so much to travel such a long way?

In this section you will be looking at a number of different sources of evidence. From them we can begin to see if religion was the only reason for going on a crusade.

Read them all carefully before answering the questions. An (S) after the source means that it was written a long time after the events that it is describing. 'S' stands for secondary source. (P) means primary source. It was written during the time of the crusades.

A A modern historian wrote this about the first crusade in 1978. From *The Wars of the Crusades*:
Poor peasants and poor Knights saw the chance to make money in land. (**S**)

B In about 1107 a writer in the *Gesta Francorum* said:
Let us unite in Christ's faith and the victory of the Holy Cross, for, God willing, today we shall all be made rich. (**P**)

C Some of the people who went on a crusade did so for some strange reasons. A French writer, Jacques de Vitry, writing in about 1230 said they were:
Thieves, robbers, pirates, singers, dice players, actors and nuns that sold their bodies to men. (**P**)

D A book by St Bernard of Clairvaux, written in 1147, gave another reason for crusading:
Evil men have begun to occupy this land. Unless someone stops them they will be feasting their eyes upon the [holiest places] of our religion. (**P**)

E From *Medieval Europe 400–1500* by H G Koeningsberger (1987):
In 1095 the Byzantine Emperor Alexius I appealed to Pope Urban II (1088–1099) for help against the Seljuk Turks in Asia Minor. (**S**)

F From a sermon by Odo of Chateauroux from about 1248:
Some say 'The Muslims have not hurt me at all. Why should I take the cross against them?' But if he thought well about it he would understand that the Muslims do great injury to every Christian. (**P**)

G A modern historian suggests some interesting reasons why going on a crusade might be a good idea. Adapted from *What Were the Crusades?* by J Riley-Smith (1977).
At the time of the First Crusade . . . pilgrims could only be brought before church courts for trial. They had to be protected from attack. Things stolen from them had to be returned. They did not have to pay taxes. Their families were protected by the church. (**S**)

H This comes from a book written in about 1148 by Anna Comnena, the daughter of Alexius I who was ruler of the Byzantine Empire. She said of the crusades:
To all appearances they were on a pilgrimage to Jerusalem; in reality they planned to dethrone Alexius and seize his capital. (**P**)

I A 14th-century picture showing some of the things that might have gone on during the crusades.

cnnam et reuerentia exhibendo pur i euâ | 7 gñr indicitur optimu est iusta 7 pec conā
gelio ſcā Joħs Apłi et euangelifte uera, | cata tam cānalia q̃ ſpũalia ciuitae cuz
ater recitatur. Siqs diligit me ſ mone. | ex eis nullum lonum comodū trahi poſ
meū ſuabit, 7 pater mñs diliget eum et meū | ſit ñ aliquis lonus fruct. Et qz terra
ad eum ueiem 7 maſione apud eum ſa | ſcā dignioz exiſtir ceteis alug ab ipſa diŭ
ciem; Qui nõ diligit me ſ mone meū | ſtantib qp ſalute humāi gñis quam
nõ ſuat. 7c. Item p pſalmiſtā. Dñe 7 | in ea redemptoz ñr tangz intre ubilico

Who Would go on a Crusade and Why?

Look at the people described below. Discuss in pairs each one, saying if you think each character would go on a crusade or not. You must give as many reasons as you can for your answer.

J A 14th-century picture showing Turks attacking Christian pilgrims.

Character	Name and age	Details	Would they go on a crusade or not?
	Jack Dell aged 35	A Frenchman born in Paris. A shoemaker but also a thief. He is suspected by his neighbour of stealing some silver rings. His mother is very religious.	
	Margaret aged 50	Very religious. Her husband has just died leaving her some money. She does not like travelling. Her family don't like her because she is very bossy but her son will do as he is told.	
	Duke of Bronnich aged 30	The youngest son of a wealthy German family. He is not very religious but knows that he will never be as rich as his father or elder brothers if he stays in Germany.	
	Edith aged 26	A nun. She has no money at all but is very religious. She does not know how to get to the Middle East. She does not like fighting but is quite strong.	

1. Put the sources in chronological order – starting with the oldest first. Write your answers as a list with the source letter and date. The first one is done for you: source B 1107.
2. Look at the sources again and say if you agree or disagree with this sentence. Explain your answer in as much detail as you can. 'Historians only use primary sources to write books'.
3. Sort out the sources on these pages under these headings. (You may want to put some sources under more than one heading.)
   (i) Reasons for crusading to do with religion or church.
   (ii) Reasons for crusading to do with wanting to make money.
   (iii) Reasons for crusading to do with taking land from the Muslims (Turks or Arabs).
4. Now look at the column with the most sources in it. Is this column the most important reason why people went on crusades? Explain your answer carefully.
5. 'No matter what historians say, most people at the time of the crusades went on them for religious reasons.' Do you agree with this? Explain your answer carefully.

Historians use sources of evidence to help them find out what went on in the past. Often they have put together information from lots of sources. This is what you will be doing in this chapter.

It was one thing deciding to travel to the East; it was quite another problem actually getting there. The First Crusade faced a long and difficult journey by land. It had to travel through Eastern Europe and then the Byzantine Empire (modern Turkey) before reaching the Muslim lands of the East.

It was a long way and could take months. Later crusaders could sail across the Mediterranean to the sea ports that had been captured. These were near to the holy places, like Jerusalem. Sailing was a faster way to travel to the East but it too had its problems, as you shall find out.

The rest of this chapter is made up of a number of different sources to do with the problems of travelling to the East.

A The Emperor Frederick Barbarossa wrote in November 1189:
Bandits attacked us from the mountain slopes throughout the wooded areas of Bulgaria.

B From the *Deeds of the Franks*, written sometime after the First Crusade (1099). We don't know who wrote it. It describes travelling across Anatolia (Turkey).
They bled their horses and asses and drank the blood. Others let down belts and clothes into a sewer and squeezed out the liquid into their mouths; others passed water into one another's cupped hands and drank.

C Odo of Deuil, writing at the time of Louis VII's crusade in 1147–1148, said
The Byzantines locked up their cities and towns, and sent down items for sale on ropes from walls. Food provided in this way was not enough for our vast army. So the pilgrims, who could not bear to go without, obtained things by plunder and pillage.

D A writer from Wurzburg in Germany describes Conrad III's journey east in 1147:
Even if the road we must take is steep and difficult, yet for God . . . we will fight the Turks . . . lead us through the pathless places which are unknown to us.

E From the *Chronicle* *of Tyre* written soon after the event described.
On 9th May 1271, Prince Edward, son of Henry III, King of England, landed in Acre, after a stormy crossing in which his ship had been struck and almost sunk by the storm. He brought his wife, Eleanor of Castile, with him.

F Soldiers of the First Crusade suffering as they travelled through Turkey. The picture was made in the 19th century.

G People from the crusade of Peter the Hermit being attacked at Nicea in Turkey by Muslim soldiers. The picture was made in the 14th century.

H A modern historian (Ronald Finucane: *Soldiers of the Faith*, 1983) said about the Sixth Crusade in Egypt, that:

Bad weather, thirst and exhaustion, made crusaders [victims] of diseases, like dysentery. One famous victim was the King of France – his dysentery made him use the [toilet] so often that his draws were cut away to simplify things.

I A chronicle written about the same time as the Third Crusade (1188–1192). This source is about King Richard sailing to Europe, across the Mediterranean Sea, from the east.

On 11th November 1192, King Richard, worn out by the long, rough sea voyage, landed at Corfu. He agreed to pay some pirates to take him to a safer place.

J A chronicle from the First Crusade. The crusade was led by Frederick Barbarossa. It describes Southern Turkey in June 1190.

At this time both rich and poor, both sick and those who seemed well, were struggling against the heat of the sun on a difficult route over rocky paths. Frederick Barbarossa tried to swim across the fast-flowing river Goksu . . . and drowned.

K A photograph taken in the Taurus mountains of southern Turkey. Most overland crusades had to pass through this area. The road is a modern one.

1 Read the sources very carefully. Then copy out the chart below and fill in the details for each source. The finished chart will give you a good idea of what travelling was like in those days. The first one has been done for you. Use only the written sources.

Source letter and who wrote it?	Primary or secondary Source?	What are the problems of travelling that it mentions?	Where do these problems take place?	What date or crusade is mentioned?
Source A Emperor Frederick Barbarossa	Primary	Attacked by bandits	Bulgaria	1189
Source B				

2 Is the following sentence true or false? Explain your answer very carefully. 'The journey to the East was *always* very difficult'.

19

| 1000 | 1050 | 1100 | 1150 | 1200 | 1250 | 1300 |

1

In the 6th and 7th Centuries AD Arab peoples took control of most of the area shown on the map. They were Muslims and encouraged the building of mosques for worship and universities for learning.

2

By the 10th Century AD the Muslim east was divided. The Abbasid dynasty ruled from Baghdad and were Sunni Muslims. The Fatimids ruled from Cairo and were Shi'ite Muslims.

8

In 1095 the Byzantine Emperor Alexius I thought it was time to attack the Muslim states of the east. He was not strong enough to do this alone. So he called on Christian countries of the west to help him fight the Muslims. Little did he know what was going to happen!

Black Sea

BYZANTINE EMPIRE

Constantinople

DANISH MENDS

SELJUKS OF RUM (TURKEY)

ARMENIANS

Aegean Sea

(GREECE)

•Antioch

Crete

Cyprus

Damascus

Mediterranean Sea

•Acre

•Jerusalem

•Cairo

FATIMIDS (EGYPT)

Red Sea

7

Besides the Seljuk Turks of Iraq and Syria and the Fatimids of Egypt, the Muslims also ruled in present day Turkey, the Seljuks of Rum in the west and the Danish mends in the east. To the south was the small, mainly Christian state of Armenians.

6

The Middle East was very wealthy; it controlled trade between Europe and the Far East. Thanks to the Arabs the region had laws, education, art but not much unity.

3

In 1040 the Seljuk Turks, who were Sunni Muslims, took control of the area, apart from Fatimid Egypt and the Byzantine Empire. In 1071 they defeated the Byzantine Emperor at the battle of Manzikert.

The names of modern countries in the region are in brackets

300ml

480km

4

The Byzantines were Eastern or Orthodox Christians.
The Byzantine Empire controlled large parts of Eastern Europe, as well as Greece, Crete and Cyprus. It was very wealthy and despite its defeat by the Turks, Constantinople, the capital, was safe behind high walls.

anzikert

GREAT SELJUKS

dessa

RIA)

(IRAQ)

• Baghdad

Disputed Area

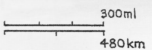

ARABIA
Nomadic Tribes

(SAUDI ARABIA)

This section gives you some idea about what the Middle East was like at the time the First Crusade set out in 1096. It gives you some clues about why the crusades went to this area and why they were able to reach, and capture, part of it.

5

The area around Antioch, Damascus, Acre and Jerusalem was disputed by Arabs and Turks. The rulers of towns and cities often fought amongst themselves. No one ruler was able to control the whole area.

1. Using a modern atlas find the names of countries in this area today.
2. Give two reasons why the Great Seljuks and the Fatimids might fight each other.
3. Write a paragraph to explain why the First Crusade might just succeed in getting to Jerusalem.
4. When the crusades arrived in the Seljuks of Rum's land they had to fight all the way. Why was this?
5. Sometimes the crusaders fought on the same side as the rulers of Muslim towns and cities in the East. Why was this? Explain your answer carefully.

| 1000 | 1050 | 1100 | 1150 | 1200 | 1250 | 1300 |

Historians often find more than one source of evidence about the same event. They need to check one source against another.

A Godfrey of Bouillon. He was to become ruler of Jerusalem.

The leader of the first group of pilgrims to leave for the East was called Peter the Hermit. He led 20,000 people from Germany to Turkey. Peter's followers were beaten by the Turks in the late summer of 1096. They had only just reached Muslim territory.

This setback did not stop crusading. By the spring of 1097 almost 10,000 people from all over Europe were gathered near Constantinople. They were ready to begin the long journey to the Middle East.

This great army is known today as the First Crusade. The Pope had put Bishop Adbenar in charge but he left most of the work to other people. So there was no one leader in command.

The crusade was made up of at least four different armies. One was led by the Frenchman, Raymond, Count of Toulouse and Provence. Another was led by Hugh of Vermandos, who was the younger brother of the King of France. Robert, Duke of Normandy, brother to King William II of England led a third. Bohemond and Tancred, Norman lords from southern Italy, brought important numbers of soldiers with them as well.

Besides these leaders there were many others in command of small numbers of soldiers. All the armies were followed by huge numbers of pilgrims.

The Byzantine Emperor Alexius had managed to persuade some of these leaders to swear an oath of loyalty to him. He hoped to use this oath to control the crusaders. He wanted to keep any territory that they won from the Turks or Arabs for himself.

The first target for the crusades was Nicea. It was an important fortress and capital of the Turkish ruler, Kilij Arslan. Luckily for the crusaders, Kilij was away fighting when they arrived. So they were able to attack the place without great loss.

By October 1097 the army had reached Antioch, one of the most important cities in the East. It was protected by strong walls and the Turks who held it were not going to give in easily. In fact it took a siege of over seven months to capture the city.

Meanwhile, crusaders went off on their own to see what they could capture. Baldwin of Boulogne was the luckiest. He managed by March 1098 to take control of a large area of land around the town of Edessa. It became known as the County of Edessa. It was the first area of the Middle East to be controlled by a crusader from the West.

B The walls of Antioch. A picture made in the 19th century based on the actual remains.

After Antioch had fallen a row broke out between Raymond, Count of Toulouse, who was the most important person on the crusade and Bohemond, who was the best military leader. They both wanted the city. In the end Raymond marched south towards Jerusalem, leaving Bohemond with the city.

C This is an extract from a ▓novel▓ called *Count Bohemond*. It was written in 1964 by Alfred Duggan.

After his hurried look at the walls Bohemond could not imagine how to capture Antioch. While that strong wall stood undamaged they could not storm it; the rising ground made it impossible to bring ▓siege engines▓ close enough to batter it. Still, if Taticius* was right the walls were very long. They might find a weak spot somewhere. Perhaps after the whole army had come up some other leader might have a bright idea.

* Taticius was a Byzantine army general. He worked for the Emperor Alexius but was helping the crusaders to get to the East.

___1___ a) What was the name of the bishop that the Pope put in charge of the First Crusade?
b) Make a list of the other leaders of the crusade and where they came from. You should have *five* names.

___2___ You don't need to write anything for this question. Using the map below find the route that the crusaders took to the Middle East.

___3___ Using the months, years and seasons mentioned in this unit make up a timeline to show the events of the First Crusade. Try to make all of it fit down one page.

___4___ a) What event is being described in source C?
b) When did this event take place?

___5___ Because source C is a novel, does this mean that it cannot be trusted to tell us about events of the First Crusade? Explain your answer carefully.

___6___ Look at the picture source B and the novel source C. Do the sources agree about the Walls of Antioch? Explain your answer.

D A map showing the route of the First Crusade.

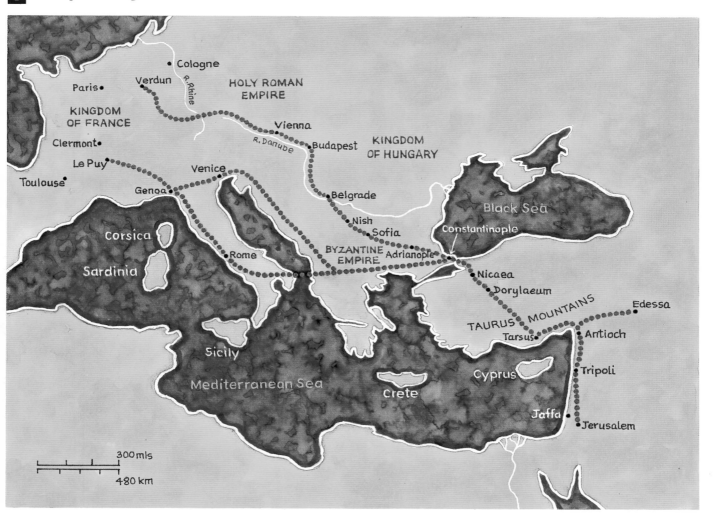

IMAGES OF THE EAST

Historians use the word *motives* to describe the reasons why people did things in the past.

Some of the things done by people in the crusades might seem very odd today. Why, for example, were people prepared to fight and die in the crusades?

We have looked at some of the reasons why people went on crusades and we have seen that Jerusalem was a very important city for Christians, Muslims and Jews. Jerusalem was thought to be so important that many people died trying to capture it. If we are to make sense of all this killing we need to know what Christians thought about Muslims and Jews.

Sources A and B show what some Christians thought about Muslims.

Some Christian traders had done business with Muslim merchants. Other Christian scholars had been to Islamic universities in Spain.

Not all of the Christians who drew or wrote about Muslims had actually met one. Most Christians didn't know much about the Islamic world. Their image or picture of Islam came partly from the words of the Pope (source C) and from other churchmen.

A Medieval Christian view of a Muslim.

B Medieval Christian view of Muslims as cannibals.

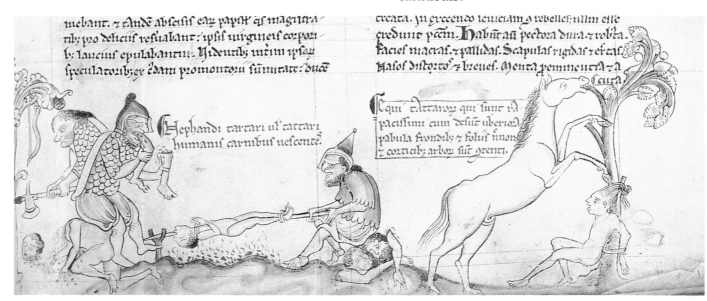

From a speech by Pope Urban II in 1095, encouraging Christians to go on a crusade to the Holy Land.

You must run as quickly as you can to help your brothers living on the eastern shores. The Turks have overrun them, slaughtering and capturing many and destroying churches. They cut open their navels, and tear out their insides. They tie them to a stake, or drag them and flog them. All men going there who die will immediately be forgiven their sins.

Many Christians also relied on stories and rumours for their knowledge of Jews. In some parts of Europe Jews had set up their own communities, living and working alongside people of other religions. In other cities Jews lived in separate quarters , away from the local Christian people.

In 1066 a number of Jews came over to England with the Norman invaders. They settled in important trading cities, such as London, Norwich, Bristol and York. Some of them became rich and powerful by lending money. Traders, nobles and even kings borrowed money from the Jews.

The crusader King, Richard I, disliked Jews. Richard did not allow Jews to take part in the coronation celebrations. Nor did he stop a crowd of people from attacking and killing some Jews who had turned up to give him a present.

In 1190 the houses of Jews were burnt in York, Norwich and Bury St Edmunds. In that same year, a York nobleman called Roger Malbis decided to settle his debts with a Jewish money lender before going on King Richard's crusade. But he did not pay the money back.

D Jews being attacked.

Instead, Malbis led an attack on the houses of the Jews of York. The terrified Jews hid in York castle. A mob set the castle on fire and some of the Jews were burnt to death.

The next day Malbis promised that the survivors would be safe if they came out. But when they did they were killed. Malbis went to York Minster and used altar candles to burn the records of all debts to the Jews. He then went off on the crusade.

Another famous crusader King, Edward I of England, treated the Jews badly. In 1275 he banned them from lending money. He raised about £16,500 by taxing the Jews. It was nearly half the total amount of money raised by his government. He also made the Jews wear a yellow badge. In 1287 Edward promised to go on another crusade. The tax on the Jews helped pay for it.

Also that year the leaders of every Jewish family were sent to the Tower of London. They were accused of trying to clip or steal coins. At least 269 Jews were hanged at the Tower. On 18 July 1290 the rest were expelled from England.

E The Christian monk Richard of Devizes described what happened in London after Richard I's coronation, 3 September 1189.

They began to sacrifice the Jews to their father the devil. Other towns and cities copied the people of London and sent these bloodsuckers down to hell. Either the Jews were roasted in their houses, or if they left their houses were killed with swords.

F The Jewish historian, Rabbi Jonathan Romain, explains how there was hatred of both Jews and the Muslims.

The crusades were difficult for the Jews. People said to themselves, 'Why are we going all the way across the Mediterranean to beat up the unbelievers over there, when we can sort them out in our own back yard first?' Many of the people going on crusades were in debt. They also felt that it was unfair that they were going to save the Holy Land from the unbelievers , when their own lands in England were under the control of the Jewish unbelievers.

1 If you only had sources A and C to go on, what would you think Muslims were like? Explain how you decided.

2 Look at sources A and B.
   a) Who produced these pictures?
   b) Do you think they are reliable? Give reasons.

3 How do you explain some of the violent things Christians did to Muslims and Jews at the time of the crusades?

1000	1050	1100	1150	1200	1250	1300

A A 15th-century painting of the siege of Jerusalem.

In the summer of 1099 crusader armies attacked and captured the holy city of Jerusalem. The crusaders thought that they had won a great victory.

Pope Urban II died in Italy two weeks after Jerusalem was taken. The good news arrived too late.

The capture of Jerusalem had been difficult. The city was defended by high walls and the crusaders were short of materials to build siege towers. They were also short of water in the very hot weather.

There were rumours that wells had been poisoned. The first attempts to capture the city were easily beaten back.

In June 1099 six ships carrying supplies arrived from Europe. A crusader called Tancred returned at the same time with logs from the forests of Samaria. By 10 July two wooden siege towers had been built. The tower at the north walls was commanded by Duke Godfrey of Lorraine; the tower at the south was commanded by Count Raymond of Toulouse. The crusaders were ready for another attack.

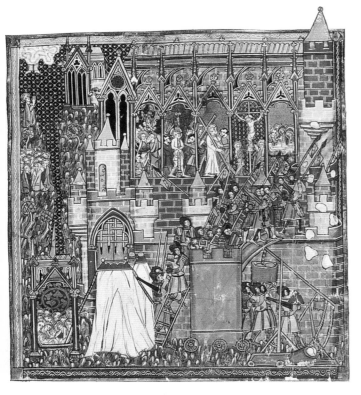

B Another version of the siege of Jerusalem by the crusaders. This one comes from a 14th-century French manuscript.

C From the *Gesta Francorum* by a monk called Fulcher of Chartres. He travelled with the crusaders and was an eye-witness to many of the events he described.

On Friday 15th July 1099, early in the morning, we attacked the city from all sides, but we could make no progress. We were all very frightened. Godfrey of Bouillon and his brother were fighting bravely in the siege tower. Then one of our knights, Lethold, climbed up onto the walls of the city.

As soon as he had climbed it, all the defenders of the city fled along the walls and through the city. Our men, following Lethold, chased after them, killing them and dismembering them. There was such slaughter that we were up to our ankles in blood.

Count Raymond of Toulouse led his army and a siege tower from the south close up to the wall. But then the emir, who was in David's Tower, surrendered to the count, and opened up the gate for him.

Our pilgrims entered the city and chased the Saracens, killing as they went. At least [unbelievers] were overcome, and our men killed whoever they wished. All the dead Saracens were cast out of the city, on account of the terrible [smell]. Nearly the whole city was crammed with their bodies. The Saracens who were still alive dragged the dead ones out in front of the gates and made huge piles of them, as big as houses.

D A modern historian, Sir Stephen Runciman, in his *History of the Crusades*, written in 1951.

It was decided that the main attack would begin during the night of 13–14th July. The main attack would be launched at the same time from Mount Sion and on the Northern Walls. The first task of the attackers was to bring their wooden castles right up to the walls. This involved the filling of the ditch which ran round their feet. By the evening of the 14th, Raymond's men had succeeded in wheeling their tower over the ditch against the wall. But the defence was fierce. Raymond could not get a foothold on the wall itself.

Next morning Godfrey's tower closed in on the North Wall. About midday they succeeded in making a bridge from the tower to the top of the wall. Two Flemish knights led the army across, followed by Godfrey himself. Scaling ladders allowed many more attackers to climb into the city. The Muslims surrendered and promised to pay a heavy ransom. All that afternoon and all night the massacre continued.

E A description of the capture of Jerusalem by the Muslim writer Ibn al-Athir. He was writing about 100 years after the event.

The Franks besieged Jerusalem for more than six weeks. They built two towers, one of which, near Sion, the Turks burnt down, killing everyone inside it. In fact the city was taken from the north on the morning of Friday 15th July. The population was killed by the Franks. They massacred over 70,000 men, among them scholars and devout hermits. They stripped the Dome of the Rock of a great deal [of] treasure.

Historians try not to rely on just one source of evidence. They compare sources to find out what happened in the past. These sources may contain different points of view.

Historians ask questions of the evidence such as:
- who made it?
- when was it made?
- why was it made?
- how reliable is it?

1 What can you tell about the siege of Jerusalem from sources A, B and C?

2 Can source A be used to check what source D says about the siege of Jerusalem? Explain your answer.

3 How useful is source C for finding out about the siege of Jerusalem?

4 What kinds of information about the siege of Jerusalem can you get in source C that you don't find in sources A and B?

5 What problems are there in using this collection of sources to explain the capture of Jerusalem?

6 Who wrote source E? How does this information affect its reliability?

1000	1050	1100	1150	1200	1250	1300

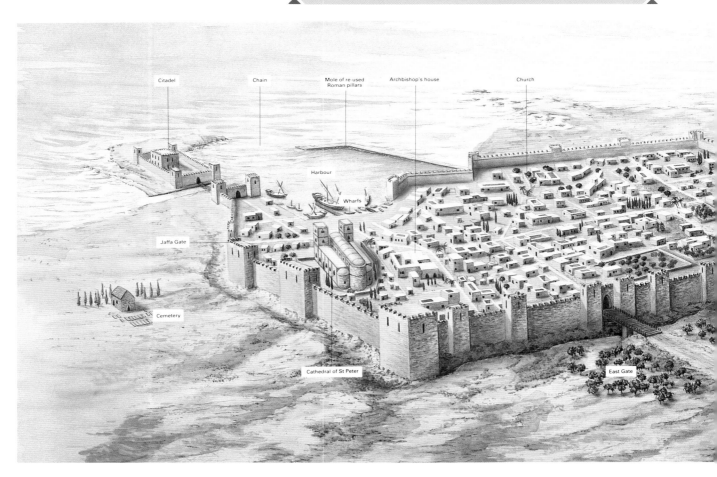

Citadel · Chain · Mole of re-used Roman pillars · Archbishop's house · Church · Harbour · Wharfs · Jaffa Gate · Cemetery · Cathedral of St Peter · East Gate

A A modern artist's impression of Caesarea in the 12th century.

In this unit think about how historians reconstruct things from the past. It might be a building, a town or a battle but all need to be based upon evidence.

Most crusaders and pilgrims to Palestine did not stay very long. They often returned to Europe as soon as a crusade was over or after visiting a few holy places. Some, however, did settle down in the East. Most Christian settlers lived in coastal towns or castles; only a few went into the countryside.

Life on the land was dangerous and difficult. Those already living in the area were usually native Syrians, many of whom were Christians, or Muslim Arabs. The dangers mainly came from hungry crusading armies that might rob and kill villagers of any religion.

Life was hard because the land was not easy to farm. The weather was very hot in the summer and there wasn't much fresh water. Travelling was difficult because roads were poor and many areas were hilly or mountainous. The country people had to pay heavy taxes to Christian or Muslim rulers alike.

Despite its dangers, a life in the East tempted many poor pilgrims, knights and wealthy merchants. The first area of the East to be controlled by crusaders (1098) became known as the County of Edessa.

It was ruled by Baldwin of Boulogne, one of the leaders of the First Crusade. Most of the Europeans who settled there lived in castles or towns. Most of the local people were Christians anyway.

South of Edessa was the principality of Antioch which was founded by Count Bohemond after a fight with the Byzantine Empire. Further south, around the important port of Tripoli, Raymond St Giles set himself up as 'Count of Tripoli'. The port itself was not captured until 1109, some years after he had died.

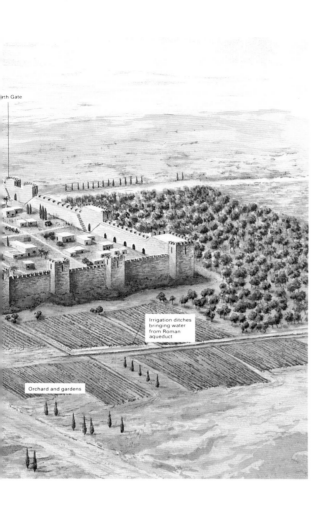

1 a) What was the first area of the East to be controlled by crusaders called?
   b) Who ruled this area?
   c) Why did the size of the crusader states change?
2 Look at the picture of Caesarea in the 12th century.
   a) Describe how Caeserea was defended.
   b) Using the map say which crusader state Caesarea was in.
   c) Make a list of the reasons why Christian pilgrims might prefer to live here rather than in the countryside.
   d) What clues in the picture suggest that Caesarea is a very ancient town?
   e) The picture of Caesarea was made by an artist in the 1980s. How did he work out what it looked like in the 12th century?
   f) Which part of Caesarea was the hardest to attack? Explain your answer carefully.

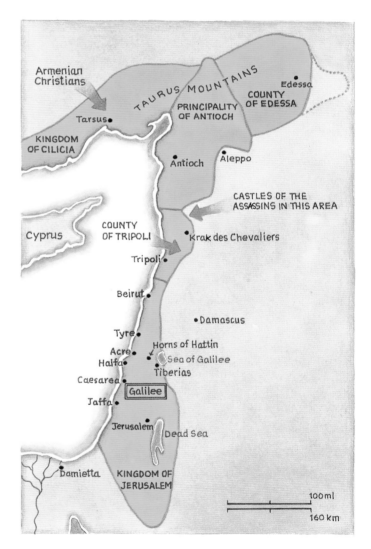

But Raymond had managed in the meantime to conquer a number of important coastal towns. These attracted the Italian merchants of Venice and Genoa. The merchants took the opportunities that the crusades offered to open up a rich trade with the East.

The largest and most powerful crusader state was the Kingdom of Jerusalem. Its first king was Godfrey of Bouillon who was elected in July 1099 by other leaders of the First Crusade. Godfrey died in 1100.

After some dispute, Baldwin of Boulogne, Godfrey's brother, became the next King of Jerusalem, leaving Edessa in the control of his cousin.

Over the next 200 years the size of the crusader states changed depending on how well the crusading armies were doing. The Christian states of the East were finally swept away by Mamluk armies from Egypt in 1291. Christian control of the East had finally come to an end.

B A map showing the crusader states in 1186. By 1190 Saladin had recaptured most of the places shown on this map.

WHO SETTLES WHERE?

The people of the Middle Ages had different ideas and attitudes from people today. They also had different ideas from each other. How did this affect the way they might have acted? This unit helps you to think about this problem.

On the page opposite is a map showing a small part of Palestine. It has been made up to help you think about some of the problems that pilgrims, crusaders, settlers and Muslims had.

Study the map and copy it into your books. Read the information around the sides, then have a go at the questions on this page in pairs.

1   You are the leader of a group of Christian knights. You want to build a castle in this area to protect Christian villages and the road to Jerusalem. Where would you build the castle? Explain your answer very carefully.

2   You are a pilgrim from Sweden (a skilled blacksmith) and decide to settle down in Palestine. Which village might you want to live in? Explain your answer carefully.

3   You are a merchant from Venice in Italy. You want to set up a cotton buying business in the area. In which village might you set up in business? (You don't like the people of Genoa and must live near the road to Acre.)

4   You are the local Muslim leader and have heard that the Christians are going to build a castle in your area. You don't like the idea. How can you try to stop them doing this?

5   A large crusading army has arrived in Acre from Europe. Its leaders want to know if it is worth attacking the castle of the local Muslim leader. What might the following people say? Explain each of your answers carefully.
a) The local Bishop – a keen crusader.
b) The merchants from Venice and Genoa from question 3.
c) The Swedish pilgrim from question 2.
d) The Christian knights living in their newly-built castle from question 1.

6   Don't forget this exercise has been made up. To find out what *real* people in the past thought and did is very much harder. Look at some of the characters mentioned in this section. Could a historian really find out about the lives of similar people living at the time? Explain your answer very carefully.

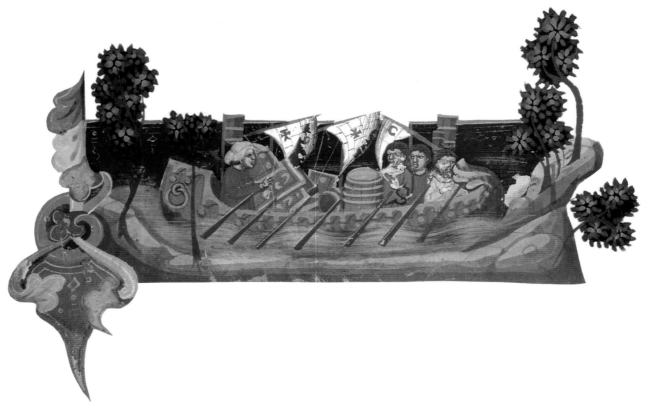

A A boat loaded with stores and supplies sailing for the Middle East.

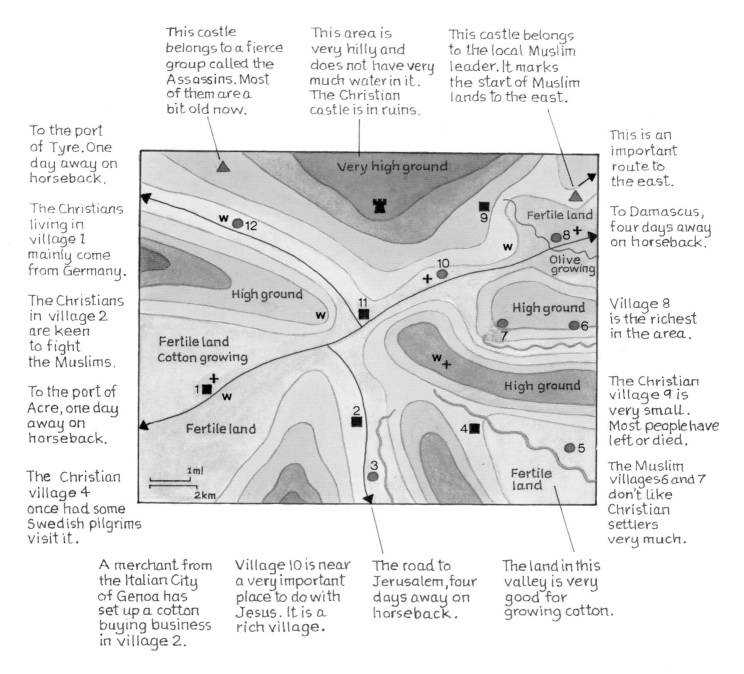

This castle belongs to a fierce group called the Assassins. Most of them are a bit old now.

This area is very hilly and does not have very much water in it. The Christian castle is in ruins.

This castle belongs to the local Muslim leader. It marks the start of Muslim lands to the east.

This is an important route to the east.

To the port of Tyre. One day away on horseback.

The Christians living in village 1 mainly come from Germany.

The Christians in village 2 are keen to fight the Muslims.

To the port of Acre, one day away on horseback.

The Christian village 4 once had some Swedish pilgrims visit it.

To Damascus, four days away on horseback.

Village 8 is the richest in the area.

The Christian village 9 is very small. Most people have left or died.

The Muslim villages 6 and 7 don't like Christian settlers very much.

Very high ground

Fertile land

Olive growing

High ground

High ground

High ground

Fertile land Cotton growing

Fertile land

Fertile land

1 ml
2 km

A merchant from the Italian City of Genoa has set up a cotton buying business in village 2.

Village 10 is near a very important place to do with Jesus. It is a rich village.

The road to Jerusalem, four days away on horseback.

The land in this valley is very good for growing cotton.

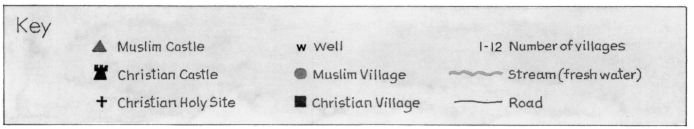

Key

▲ Muslim Castle   w Well   1-12 Number of villages

♜ Christian Castle   ● Muslim Village   〰 Stream (fresh water)

✝ Christian Holy Site   ■ Christian Village   — Road

| 1000 | 1050 | 1100 | 1150 | 1200 | 1250 | 1300 |

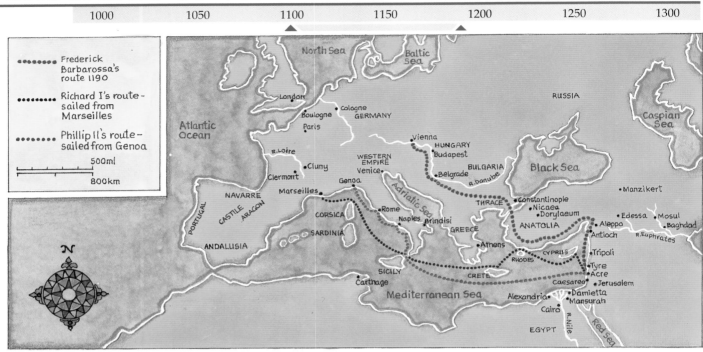

A The route of the Third Crusade.

To reach the East crusaders had to travel hundred of miles. The route crusaders took needs to be studied by historians to understand the problems they faced.

The capture of Jerusalem did not bring about the end of crusading. There were still lots of important places in Palestine that were under Muslim control. So between 1100 and 1129 at least three other crusades took place.

By 1140 the crusaders controlled a long strip of land on the east coast of the Mediterranean; it stretched from the Red Sea in the south to the mountains of what is now central Turkey. It was not going to be easy to defend because the Muslims were determined to take it back.

By the end of 1144 the area around Edessa, in the north, had been recaptured by the Muslims. This event led directly to what is now called the Second Crusade. It was a total failure.

Between 1157 and 1184 the Pope called at least seven times for another crusade to be organised but nothing very much happened. Was crusading over?

No! Because a Kurd named Salah al-Din Yusuf (we call him Saladin) united most of the Muslim East. He began to reconquer lost Muslim land.

Saladin destroyed a Christian army at the Battle of Hattin in July 1187 and captured the King of

Jerusalem. Europe was stunned, but worse was to follow. In October 1187 Saladin and his army marched into Jerusalem. Pope Urban III is said to have died of shock when he heard the news.

The new Pope, Gregory VIII, set about organising a crusade straight away. This crusade is known as the Third Crusade. When it set out in 1190 it was led by the most powerful leaders in Europe at that time. From Germany came the Emperor Frederick Barbarossa. From France came King Philip II and from England King Richard I.

Frederick and his army marched across Europe, but while crossing a small river in present-day Turkey, the 70-year-old Emperor drowned. His shocked army broke up. Only a part of it marched on to the East.

---

1 What was the name of the leader who united Muslim people in the East?

2 a) Which Pope died of shock?
b) Why did he die of shock?

3 On the map above look at the routes of the crusading armies. Using the work you have done about 'Travelling East' (pages 18–19), write a paragraph about the following things: (a) the advantages and disadvantages of travel by land; (b) the advantages and disadvantages of travel by sea.

B Women help besiege a castle, from the *Universal History* made in Jerusalem in the 13th century.

Events of the Third Crusade

Richard I and Philip II meanwhile had been organising fleets of ships to take them from Europe to the East. They set out in the summer of 1190 and stopped at the island of Sicily. In March 1191 Philip then sailed directly to Acre. Richard stopped at Cyprus and captured the island from its ruler. He eventually arrived at Acre in June 1191.

Acre had been under siege by the Christians for almost two years. With fresh soldiers Acre was captured in July 1191. It had been hard work taking Acre. King Philip was worn out and ill so he returned home. But Richard and the rest of the crusaders wanted to retake Jerusalem. So in August they marched south.

Richard's army was ready to fight, if Saladin attacked. He did. At the Battle of Arsur (Arsuf) on 7 September 1191 Richard's army beat off the Muslims.

In September 1191 Richard reached the town of Jaffa. After rebuilding it he marched on Jerusalem. It was December and the weather was wet and cold. Richard soon realised that his army was not large enough to take and hold the city, so he returned to Jaffa.

In June 1192 Richard advanced on Jerusalem once more. He saw the city but again returned to the coast.

Saladin had attacked and captured most of Jaffa in August 1192. Richard managed to recapture the city and organise a   truce   with Saladin. Neither side liked it very much but everyone was worn out. On 9 October 1192 Richard I sailed for Europe. He never returned to the East.

---

4   Do you think that the Third Crusade was a success? Explain your answer very carefully.

5   a) Look at source B. What can you find out about:
(i)   weapons and armour in the 13th century;
(ii) the part played by women in sieges?
b) Is there anything about the way the women are shown in source B which suggests that women didn't always take part in sieges?

6   It is not always easy to find out about the part played by women in the crusades. Women aren't mentioned very much. Think about why this may be and try to write a short paragraph about it.

We have seen that Richard I played an important part in the Third Crusade, but how much do we really know about him?

> This section is about the use of historical sources. You can see that the sources don't always agree with each other. Historians try to make sense of the sources by asking questions about them.

In this chapter you'll be asked to work in pairs. Your task is to look carefully at the sources that follow and to present a picture of what you think Richard was really like. Whatever you draw or write must be backed up by at least one of the sources.

Make sure you work together and both of you do some writing and drawing. You can also make up history questions such as 'Why have you given him a beard?' to ask other pairs when they do their presentation.

B A modern artist's impression of Richard I.

C From *The Journeys of King Richard* – a history written at the time of the Third Crusade.

He was tall in   stature , of shapely build, with hair between red and yellow. His limbs were straight and flexible, his arms somewhat long, he had long legs.

D Richard I as he is shown on the cover of a Ladybird book.

E From a Ladybird book about Richard I, written by L Du Garde Peach (1965).

Richard was not a good king. He cared only for his soldiers. But he was brave, and loved a brave man.

A Richard I (on the left) in Italy, 1190, from a French manuscript made in about 1350.

F An actor playing Richard I in a film.

G From *The Medieval Scene,* a children's history book by R J Unstead (1962).

Richard of England, a red-haired giant, generous, incredibly brave, hot-tempered and tactless , won a great reputation in the capture of Acre, but quarrelled with his allies who left him and went home.

H Richard I, painted by a monk called Matthew Paris in 1240.

I Written by the Islamic writer Baha' ad-Din Ibn Shaddad, during the Third Crusade.

A very powerful man, of great courage and spirit. He fought great battles and showed a burning passion for war. The king was indeed a man of wisdom, experience, courage and energy . . . excitable, brave and clever.

J Richard I from a book made in 1200.

1 a) Make a drawing of what you think Richard looked like.
b) Around it write words or phrases which describe his character – what kind of person he was and what he looked like.
c) Present your ideas to the rest of the class.

2 Are these statements true or false? Explain your answers carefully.
a) 'Pictures are much better than words at telling us what people in the past were like.'
b) 'Nobody knows what Richard looked like.'
c) 'Sources made nearest the time of Richard I are always better than those made later.'
d) 'Historians don't need to know what Richard looked like but they do need to know what kind of person he was.'

A Picture of a jousting match between Richard and Saladin. They never actually met. The picture was made in Western Europe. (Date unknown.)

We have seen that Saladin won battles against the crusaders and captured towns from them. He had pictures painted and stories written about him by artists and writers from both sides.

What was Saladin really like? What sort of a person was he? If you look at the picture of him you may see that there is an obvious problem in finding out about Saladin.

Different sources provide different information. This is not only true of written sources. It is also true of pictures. Some give a different impression from others. Historians ask *who* wrote or made the sources, as well as *why* they were written or made.

B A portrait of Saladin by an Egyptian artist. It may have been painted whilst Saladin was still alive. We don't know if the artist met Saladin.

C Saladin orders the prisoners to be chained, by a European artist, date unknown.

D A description of Saladin in a book about King Richard I. It was written in the early 13th century by a canon in London.

Saladin made a disgraceful income out of the prostitutes of Damascus. None of them could carry on her filthy trade without first buying a licence from him. He spent the money on entertainers. That king of the brothels, who fought in the taverns, and spent his time gambling.

He conquered countries either by trickery or force. But the greedy tyrant concentrated all his efforts on an attempt to seize the Holy Land, Palestine.

E This is from a biography of Saladin by the Muslim Baha' ad-Din Ibn Shaddad. He travelled with Saladin.

Saladin did not spend a single gold or silver coin on anything except jihad [holy war]. Out of his desire to fight for God's cause he left behind his family, children, country, home and all the towns under his control.

Saladin was well-mannered and entertaining. If anyone was sick he would ask about his illness, his treatment, food and drink and whether there was any change in his condition. I never saw him insult anyone. He always stuck to his word and was loyal. No orphan ever came to him without Saladin offering to provide the same amount of care as his father had done. He treated old people kindly and generously.

F A description of Saladin in a modern history book called *Chronicle of the Crusades*, edited by Elizabeth Hallam (1989).

Saladin used the idea of jihad [holy war] to bring the Muslims together. His popularity with the poor people increased when he survived several assassin attacks.

Friends and enemies saw Saladin as a man of honour. Even the crusaders praised him. However, he was criticised for fighting against his fellow Muslims and for failing to capture Tyre. Nevertheless Saladin continues to be admired today.

---

1 Read source D. Find two opinions about Saladin.

2 Look at the three pictures of Saladin.
   a) What differences do you notice?
   b) Why do you think the pictures are so different?
   c) Which of the pictures do you trust *least* as evidence of what Saladin looked like? Explain your answer.

3 Which of the pictures do you trust *most* as evidence of what Saladin looked like? Explain your answer.

4 Using all the sources, write your own character sketch of Saladin.

LATER CRUSADES AT A GLANCE

The Fourth Crusade

In 1198 Pope Innocent III called for a new crusade.

It was led by some French noblemen.

It was going to Egypt on ships from Venice (Italy).

Instead of going to Egypt the crusade went to Constantinople to help Alexius IV to get his throne back.

In 1203 the crusaders took the city for Alexius. Then in the spring of 1204 they took it for themselves and split up the Byzantine Empire. Count Baldwin became Emperor.

The Fifth Crusade

In 1213 Pope Innocent III called for a crusade to the east.

Duke Leopold of Austria, King Andrew of Hungary and King Hugh of Cyprus reached Acre by sea in 1217.

They fought some battles with the Muslims in Palestine 1217-1218. King Andrew went home in 1218.

More crusaders arrived from Europe. They decided to invade Egypt because the Sultans of Egypt were the biggest threat as they controlled most of the east.

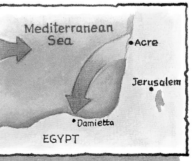

In May 1218 the crusaders sailed to Egypt and captured some land around the town of Damietta.

In July 1221 they marched south, down the River Nile, but were defeated and returned to Europe.

At this point there were so many small groups of crusaders setting out to places in the Middle East that it becomes even harder to number them. From now on they are often named after the most important person taking part.

The Crusades of Louis IX

In December 1244 Louis IX (of France) promised to go on a crusade to the east. He sailed to Egypt in August 1248.

The crusaders made a base around Damietta. In 1250 they marched south down the Nile but were defeated.

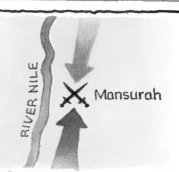

Louis was captured but paid to be set free. He spent four years in the east before returning to Europe. In 1267 he organised another crusade.

In July 1270 the crusade set out. It went to North Africa first, but many crusaders died of disease, including Louis IX. Only a few ever made it to the east.

1 Using *all* the information you have read so far begin to draw out and fill in a chart like the one below. You will need to have looked at a few crusades before you can start it, but fill it in as you read about others. We have already filled in the 'Peasants' Crusade' to give you some idea about what to write. Don't worry if you cannot always fill in the columns.

Take up quite a lot of space for this because it is important.

Once you have filled in the chart with as many crusades as you can, answer the questions below. They are all to do with the chart.

2 Who led the Peasants' Crusade?

3 a) Did crusades set out as soon as they were announced? Give examples.

b) If you put 'no' to the last question, explain carefully why they might not be able to set out straight away.

What was the name or number of the crusade?	What date was it announced?	When did it set out?	Who led the crusade?	How and where did it go?	Do you think that it was a success? Explain your answer.
The Peasants' Crusade	1095	1096	Peter the Hermit	It went by land, to Nicaea in present day Turkey.	No, the crusade was destroyed by the Turks. It never got anywhere near Jerusalem.
The First Crusade					

1 Spain

By AD 718 most of Spain had been conquered by the Muslims. Only the north remained under Christian control.

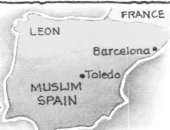

Under the leadership of the Kings of Leon the Muslims were put under continued pressure from AD 850 onwards.

1095 The Christian kings of Leon and Aragon had reconquered more than half of Spain and Portugal.

All these events occurred before Pope Urban II called the First Crusade against the Muslims in Spain as well as the east.

Although they did get some help from other Christians in Europe, it was left to the kings of Portugal, Leon, Castile, Aragon and Navarre to do the fighting.

1275 The only Muslim area left was the Kingdom of Granada in the south.

2 The Baltic

Crusades were not only directed against Muslims. In the 13th century areas of north eastern Europe around the Baltic Sea were pagan.

By the 1190s the Christian kings of northern Europe were encouraged to crusade against them.

Fighting the pagans was often done by the military orders. These were knights who were also monks. The most famous of these were the Teutonic Knights.

1250 The Teutonic Knights and other military orders had taken control of what today we call Estonia and Latvia.

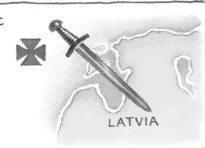

Once land had been taken by the Christian knights, settlers from Germany and Denmark were encouraged to live in the region.

1386 Lithuania became a Christian country. Up until that time the Teutonic Knights were allowed to go to war against it every year.

3 Southern France

The Cathars were a group of people that thought of themselves as Christians but believed that there were two gods.

GOD OF THE SPIRIT

GOD OF THE EARTH

They mainly lived in the mountains of south western France, where their ideas became popular with all kinds of people.

By 1200 the Pope was very worried that the Cathars' ideas were unchristian. So in 1208 Pope Innocent III declared a crusade against them.

In 1209 the crusade set out from Lyon. In July it took the town of Beziers. 15,000 Cathars and Catholics were killed. The crusade moved deep into Cathar areas.

Simon de Montfort, a **warlike** baron, was given control of the area and over the next few years crusaded against the Cathars every summer.

Despite Simon's efforts the Cathars had not been destroyed. In fact it took all the powers of the Christian Church to force the Cathars out of France (1324)

FRANCE

---

1 Is it true to say that crusades were always led by kings? Explain your answer.

2 What things stopped crusades from being a success? Make a list.

3 Historians are interested in how things change. Can you see any changes taking place in the history of crusading? (Think about: where they went to; how they got there; how successful they were.)

A Human heads are fired into a city during a siege.

The crusades were not just a set of battles. Much of the fighting has been called *siege warfare*. In a siege one side spends time trying to capture the enemy's town, fort or castle. The other side defends itself as well as it can. If you look at sources A and B you can see some of the things done by attacking and defending sides during the crusades.

What did siege warfare involve and why did it seem to suit both sides in the crusades?

Sometimes the attacking side used a giant tree trunk called a *battering ram* and tried to smash down the doors or gates of the city. Stones, nasty liquids and even beehives were thrown down onto the attackers. Tall scaling ladders were placed next to the walls in the hope that the attackers could climb into the city.

Massive catapult machines called *ballistas* and *mangonels* hurled stones at city walls. Richard I brought a huge boulder from Italy and it killed 20 people when it was fired at a city. Sometimes the attacking side simply waited outside the city walls and tried to starve the enemy into giving themselves up.

Sometimes the siege ended in a peaceful way. On other occasions it ended violently. When Jerusalem was captured by the crusaders a large number of Muslims were killed. Christian writers told the bloodthirsty story. One writer mentions crusader knights who waded through blood which came up to their ankles. The man who wrote source F claimed that the blood came up to the crusaders' knees!

Peter the Hermit's followers were accused of chopping up the babies of their enemies. Each side also accused their enemies of scalping captured soldiers. William of Tyre wrote that some crusader prisoners were sawn apart, others were buried alive or used as targets for archery practice. The crusaders are said to have taken 500 captured Muslim heads back to the camp. About 200 of them were fired into the city. Others were put on spikes.

In 1150 the crusaders at Marash were told that their lives would be spared if they surrendered – but when they gave in they were murdered. In 1191 King Richard I ordered that a large number of Muslims taken prisoner at the siege of Acre should be killed. You can read about this in sources D and E. The same thing was done to Christian prisoners by Muslims 100 years later.

B A siege during the Third Crusade.

C Crusaders fighting with Egyptian Muslims at the siege of Damietta, 1218.

The end of a siege

D A description of the killing of Muslim prisoners after the end of the siege in 1191. It was written by a Frankish Christian called Ambroise.

Two thousand seven hundred, all in chains, were led outside the wall, where they were slaughtered every one. We thank God for this!

E A description of the same event as source D. This was written by Beha ed-Din, a friend of Saladin. It comes from his book about the life of Saladin.

They brought out the Muslim prisoners. God had decided that they would become   martyrs   that day. More than three thousand were tied together with ropes and then killed. The Franks rushed at them all at once and slaughtered them in cold blood.

F A description of Jerusalem after it had been captured by crusaders. It was written by Raymond of Aguilers. He was the private chaplain to an important crusader and went on the crusade. This is an eye-witness account. His book includes lots of stories of miracles and holy visions.

It was a just and splendid judgement of God that this place should be filled with the blood of the unbelievers. The city was filled with dead bodies and blood.

Eye-witnesses are people who actually see the events they describe. This does not mean that we can always trust them more than other types of evidence. So historians often look for more than one kind of source about an event. They try to check one source against another.

1 a) What is a siege?
   b) What can you tell about sieges from source B?

2 Copy out the grid below and fill it in. One example has been done for you already.

Way of attacking	How was it supposed to work?	How could you defend against it?
Battering ram	Attackers would try to smash down the gates or doors with a massive tree trunk	Drop stones or pour nasty liquids on the attackers. You might also build extra gates, ditches or moats

3 a) Which of the ways of attacking was the best? Give reasons.
   b) Which was the worst? Give reasons.

4 Why might it suit: (a) the attacking side, and (b) the defending side to have a siege rather than a battle?

Quote from the sources in your answers to the next two questions.

5 a) Read sources D and E. On what facts do they disagree?
   b) Write down one opinion from source D and one from source E.
   c) Why are the accounts so different?
   d) On what do the two sources agree?

6 a) How can you tell from source D that it was written by a Christian?
   b) How can you tell that source E was written by a Muslim?
   c) What would you need to know about the writers to decide how reliable these sources are?

The Templars and the Hospitallers were two groups of knights who were both fighting men and monks. This was an odd mix because monks, priests and other church people were not really supposed to fight. They were not the only military orders to be formed as a result of the crusades but they are the most famous.

The Templars were founded by a French knight called Hugh of Payns in 1118–1119. Their job was to protect the pilgrim routes to Jerusalem. Hugh had some powerful supporters and was allowed to set up his headquarters in the area around the old temple in Jerusalem. This is how the order got its name.

The Hospitallers became a military order in 1130. They ran hospitals to help sick and injured pilgrims. Their most important job soon became protecting Palestine from attack. Like the Templars, Hospitallers were given land in the East and in Europe which made them very rich and powerful. The Templars and Hospitallers were fine fighting men who could always be relied upon to fight hard for the Christian cause.

However, defending Christians from attack was expensive. It meant that large castles had to be built. These cost the orders a lot of money.

In the end the Templars were destroyed by the French King Philip IV who was worried about the ideas and power they had. He burnt to death a Templar leader in March 1314.

The Hospitallers continued as a powerful military order for many years, defending Rhodes against the Turks. They did not surrender until 1522. The Hospitallers still survive today. They no longer fight, but they still care for the sick. We know them as the St John's Ambulance Brigade.

The Muslim countries of the East never had groups quite like the Templars or Hospitallers. But they did have the Assassins. This group of fanatical Muslims had castles in Northern Iran and Syria. They were famous for their carefully planned murders of important people in the East. They gave their name to a way of killing that has, sadly, become familiar to us today. They were feared by Muslims and Christians alike and were only finally defeated by the Mongols in 1256.

A A Knight Templar. From a wall painting at the Templar church in Cressoc, France. Made in the early 13th century.

B A Knight Hospitaller. A modern picture of a Hospitaller showing what they might have looked like in the late 13th century.

C An Assassin. A modern picture of an Assassin at work. They always used daggers to kill their victims.

D From *Armies of the Crusades*, by Terence Wise, (1978).

By the 1140s, the Templars were playing an important role in the military defence of the kingdom, and after mid-century the Templars and Hospitallers formed a large part of the royal army in the field. Recruits and money flowed into these two great orders and by the last quarter of the century they were the chief land owners in Outremer (the Christian east). Their knights were entrusted with the safe keeping of the greatest and most important castles in the land, and the network of communications in the Holy Land was policed by their patrols. By the early 13th century they formed half of any Christian army.

The precise number of soldiers supplied by the military orders is unknown. For the Egyptian campaign of 1158 the Hospitallers contributed 500 knights . . . The Templars agreed to supply 500 knights and mercenaries to assist King Amalric (1163-74) in return for grants of land. By the mid-13th century the Templars and Hospitallers could field only 200 and 300 knights each, although a small number must have remained in the various castles and should be added to the total strength.

E From *Chronicles of the Crusades*, edited by Elizabeth Hallam (1989).

The object of the Assassins' aggression was not the Christians, but the Shi'ite Muslims . . . They hired their services to the highest bidder, and their most famous victims include the vizier Al-Adil and Caliph al-Adil in Egypt, Raymond II of Tripoli, Conrad of Montferrat, Albert Patriarch of Jerusalem, and Philip of Montfort. Others who survived attacks were the sultans Nurod-Din and Saladin.

1 a) Who founded the Knights Templar?
b) What were the main duties of the Templars and Hospitallers?

2 Look at sources A and B. What differences can you see between the two pictures? Try to explain some of them in your own words.

3 Compare the picture of the Assassin with the Christian knights. Explain carefully why the Assassins looked so different from the Christian knights.

4 Is this sentence true or false? Explain your answer carefully. 'The Assassins only killed other Muslims.'

5 The Templars and Hospitallers were famous for their fighting skills and bravery. Try to explain in your own words why this was the case.

EFFECTS OF THE CRUSADES

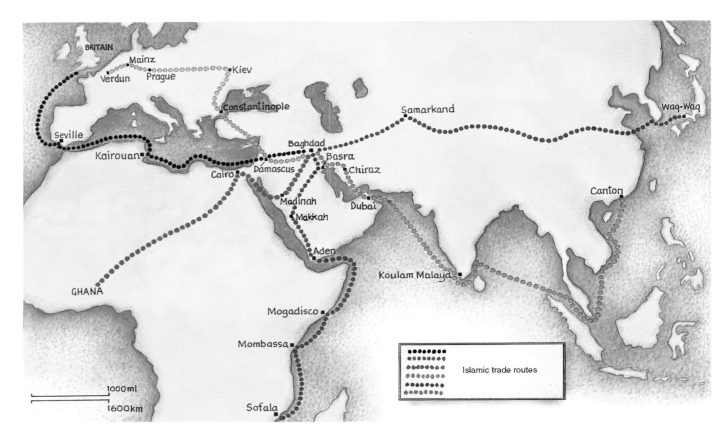

Islamic trade routes in the 10th century (before the crusades).

What happens when two very different civilisations clash? Does one side force its view of the world on the other or is the way of life of each civilisation changed? How do you decide if the crusades changed anything?

Before the crusades took place Islamic trade was established over a vast area, shown in source A.

Historians try to work out how things changed in the past. Sometimes the changes are very clear and obvious. On other occasions the pattern of change is more complicated. Old ideas and beliefs sometimes survive alongside new changes.

Historians use the word **continuity** to describe these things which stay the same. In the case of the crusades try to decide how much change they brought to Muslim lands – and how many things remained very much the same, unchanged by the crusades. Historians often disagree about how much change and how much continuity there was.

Before the crusades only a few Christian pilgrims and merchants travelled to Muslim lands. The Christian and Islamic worlds were separate. Many Muslims called all Europeans 'Rum' (Romans). The crusades brought trade as well as fighting. Some Muslim soldiers met Christians and talked to them. Other Muslims began to trade with Christian Europe.

The periods of peace in the crusades lasted much longer than the periods of war. Overall the crusades lasted for centuries, but for much of the time there was very little fighting between Christians and Muslims. Traders made use of the periods of peace. Crusaders, sailors, businessmen and pilgrims went back to Europe and wanted the goods they had seen in the Middle East.

Muslims who traded in goods such as silk, gold, iron, soap and glass did well from the contacts with Europe. It wasn't all one-way traffic.

European goods such as linen and woollen cloth became popular in parts of the Muslim world. The historian Henri Lammens wrote that the crusader conquest of Syria brought wealth to many Muslim lands around the Mediterranean Sea.

International trade helped the different rulers of some of the Muslim lands. The Mamluks, for example, built some huge and beautiful mosques. Some of the building was paid for by selling goods abroad.

Most of the people who lived in Muslim lands were not traders but farmers. Many of these people had little contact with the crusaders. The crusaders who conquered part of Syria were not the first foreigners to rule over the local farmers.

In some towns there was savage fighting. Other towns surrendered without a fight. When the crusaders lost a town to the Muslims, they often agreed to leave it altogether, so the impact they made on the town didn't last very long.

The failure of the crusades led to an increase in missionary work. Christians were unable to take back Jerusalem by force, so from the early 13th century onwards they sent missionaries to Muslim lands, in the hope that Muslims might become Christians. The first church built by the crusaders was St Paul of Tarsus, finished about 1102. After the crusaders left the area some of their churches were turned into mosques.

The Hospitaller Knights wore the badge of St. John. This has now become the badge of the St. John's Ambulance Brigade.

B A modern historian explains how the crusades affected non-Muslims who lived in Muslim lands. From *Islam from the Prophet Muhammad to the Capture of Constantinople*, edited by Bernard Lewis (1974).

The non-Muslims did well under Muslim rule, and even made an important contribution to Islamic civilisation. As long as non-Muslims accepted their position they were not troubled. The rare outbreaks of violence directed against them were usually caused by Christians or Jews gaining powerful jobs which the Muslims thought were rightfully theirs.

The position of the non-Muslims became worse during and after the crusades and the Mongol invasions, partly because of religious rivalry, and partly because of the suspicion that they were working with the enemies of Islam.

C From *The Cambridge History of Islam* edited by P M Holt (1970).

In Arabic writing of the period of the crusades, the terms crusade and crusader are missing. For the Muslim historians, the crusaders are always 'the Franks'.

The main group in the crusading states were the Franks – with three main groups, of barons, clergy and merchants. Under them was the mass of the population, consisting of Muslims, Christians and some Jews. During the conquest the Muslim population of many towns was slaughtered. The villages, however, remained, and the Franks allowed their subjects special treatment. By 1184 a Muslim traveller said that Muslim peasants were far better treated under Frankish than under Muslim rule.

D Leaders of Christian and Muslim armies meet during a break in the fighting (date unknown).

These questions ask you to think about the changes brought by the crusades to Muslim lands. Support your answers with evidence from the sources.

1 a) Make a list of the changes brought by the crusades to Muslim lands.
   b) Which things didn't change much?
   c) Who benefited from the crusades and why?
   d) Who didn't benefit from the crusades and why?
   e) Which do you think was the most important change brought about by the crusades? Give reasons for your choice.

2 In your view, how much effect do you think the crusades had on Muslim lands? Give reasons for your answer.

CHANGES IN CASTLE BUILDING

Historians try to understand what causes things to change. They also need to find out the results or consequences of those changes.

If you look at the pictures on these pages you can see that castles changed, but what caused those changes and how would you go about proving it?

We can investigate these questions by looking at some of the castles built by King Edward I of England. Between 1270 and 1272 he went on a crusade and saw a number of forts and castles. When he returned home he built a series of castles as part of his plan to control Wales. Was there a 'blueprint' of a crusader castle which was copied, or were the castles very different?

In 1277 Edward I went to war with the Welsh princes and founded several castles.

At Caernarfon Castle the ground was suitable for building secret tunnels for archers to fire from. The keep at Flint seems to have been specially designed with the comfort of the residents in mind. Rhuddlan Castle (source D) also had special features, such as a garden for the queen. This was more to do with comfort than warfare.

Conwy and Caernarfon both had high walls and many towers. Both of them were built by the sea, but one was on a rock and had no gatehouses, while the other was on low ground and had two gatehouses.

Caernarfon had very unusual striped walls. The style of these is like the style of the Roman walls at Constantinople. In 1283 Edward I had been involved in re-burying the body of Magnus Maximus, who was thought to be the father of the Roman Emperor Constantine. Imperial eagles were placed on the top of the Eagle Tower at Caernarfon.

Much of the building work at these Welsh castles was supervised by James of St George from Savoy in France. He had built crusader castles. He used sloping scaffolds when building castles. This method is thought to have been used by French and Welsh masons, but not by English ones.

A Motte and bailey castle. Many castles in Europe at the time of the First Crusade probably looked like this. Over the next 200 years people didn't completely stop building castles like this. They were usually fairly cheap and easy to build.

B Harlech Castle, 1285–90.

C From *Medieval Castles* by C Cairns (1988).
Historians used to suggest that most of the ideas for improving castles were brought by crusaders returning from the Holy Land, where they had learnt how to plan castles more scientifically.

At first the crusaders had not been so short of men, and their castles were simple; but the later castles included so many improvements that in the late 12th century they were easily the strongest in the world.

Most of these improvements seem to have been used around the eastern Mediterranean before they appeared in Europe. But there is no definite proof that it was a case of straight copying. European builders could have invented and adapted to suit the needs of whatever castle they were building.

Every site had its own advantages and problems. Even if the architect had heard about the ideas used in the latest crusader castles, he had to decide whether they could be fitted into his plans.

D Rhuddlan Castle from the air.

E From *The Medieval and Renaissance World* edited by E Wright (1979).
Domestic and church architecture, except in Spain, were not changed very much by contact with Muslims. The opposite was the case with military architecture. Before the crusades, European castles were usually little more than a single square stone tower, perhaps set on a mound, and surrounded by a wall and moat.

In Syria and Palestine the military orders learnt to build much stronger and more elaborate castles. In these the main fortifications were enclosed by a series of circular walls, all set with rounded turrets.

In England King Edward I, who had seen the castle at Acre, ordered the building of such castles at Harlech, Conwy and Caernarfon to control the conquered Welsh.

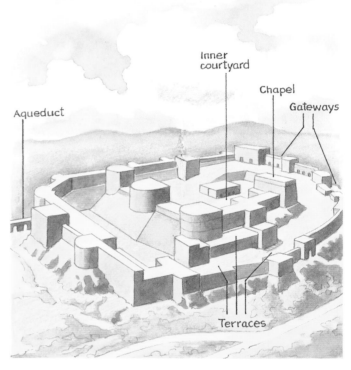

F Plans of the crusader castle, Krak des Chevaliers, Syria.

1 a) Use sources A and B to explain how castles changed.
   b) Compare sources A and D. What had not changed?
2 Look at castles D and F. Is there any common pattern? Support your answer with diagrams.
3 How important were the crusades in causing changes in castle building in Europe? Give as much evidence as you can to support your answer.

EFFECTS ON EUROPE

The crusades helped bring about more contact between Christians and Muslims. How did this contact affect Europe?

Christians borrowed some of the building styles and ideas of Muslim architects. Muslim architects built pointed arches in their mosques at least 200 years before these arches were introduced into some of the great cathedrals of Europe. The Muslims were also experts at building domes and minarets . Some European architects found it easier to build tall church towers because they knew something about the way in which Islamic minarets were built.

Islamic technology helped Europeans in a number of other ways. Islamic sailors were expert navigators . They went on long trading voyages. They needed skills to work out the direction of Makkah for daily prayer. European sailors are thought to have used a number of Islamic navigational instruments.

Clever scientists and inventors produced other pieces of technology which were useful to Europeans. Water wheels and water clocks were important inventions.

The crusaders gave European traders and businessmen a chance to get rich. Men from the Italian cities of Venice, Genoa and Florence were very successful. Woollen goods were transported from England, France, Flanders and Italy to an Italian port such as Venice and then by ship to Syria or Egypt. Italian merchants were also allowed to live in Muslim cities such as Cairo and Damascus.

Some of these merchants returned to Italy with new ideas and new ways of looking at the world. Some of them spent large amounts of money on the latest clothes, paintings, building, sculpture and so on. The crusades provided work for many people.

Farming was changed by the crusades.

Melons, apricots, rice, lemons, dates, ginger and many other foods were brought back from Muslim lands by crusaders. They also brought back knowledge about plants, irrigation and the breeding of animals.

A   Mihrab   wall from the tomb of Mustafa Pasha, Cairo, 1269–73.

B   East window of Gloucester Cathedral, about 1351.

An Islamic surgeon treated the 14th-century crusader John of Joinville. The books of Islamic doctors and scientists like Avicenna were used in European universities in the centuries after the crusades.

Many crusaders studied the Arabic language, but there is no record of the name of a Syrian or Egyptian Muslim who learnt Latin or French. Books on scientific, technical and other subjects were translated from Arabic into Latin, but we don't know of any Latin or French book which was translated into Arabic. Arabic clothes and foods became more popular amongst Europeans, but we don't know of any Arabs who preferred European food or European clothes at the time of the crusades.

C Did the crusades create another barrier between Muslims and Christians? A modern Islamic writer explains how the crusades affected the opinions held by some Christians about Islam. From *Letter to Christendom* by Rana Kabbani (1989).

The effect [of the crusades] was to produce a devilish view of Islam and its Prophet. Writer after writer repeated old lies about Muhammed, that he was an epileptic , that he smeared himself with lipstick and drenched himself in perfume. He was called the 'deceiver' and even the 'Devil' himself. Islam was described in a negative and hateful way.

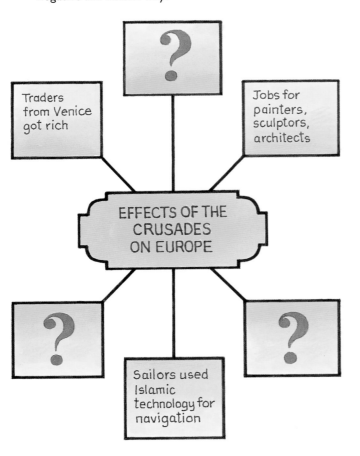

D 15th-century painting of Islamic astronomers at work. The men with the largest turbans are using an astrolabe .

1 a) Copy and complete the diagram to show the different effects of the crusades on Europe.
   b) Add any other effects you can find in the next two pages.
   c) Some of the effects are to do with technology. Shade them in blue.
   d) Can the effects be grouped under any other headings? Use other colours and show them on the key to your diagram. Don't worry if some effects need to be shaded in more than one colour.
   e) Which effect do you think was most important? Explain how you decided.

2 a) Explain two long-term effects of the crusades.
   b) Which do you think was the most important effect? Explain your answer carefully.

3 Look back over the last chapter. Did the crusades have more effect on Europe or on Muslim lands? Give as many reasons as you can.

So many things happened in the past that it is not often easy to decide which ones are important. Different historians can quite easily come up with timelines that show different dates as being important. Why is this?

A Baldwin I being crowned King of Jerusalem in 1100. He was the second Christian crusader to become ruler of the city.

In this unit you are asked to think about the dates and events that are put into timelines. There are so many possible things to put into a timeline that it is important to know why historians choose the ones that they do.

Below are two timelines on the crusades. They come from different history books. We have ended them both in 1191–1192, each really goes on a bit longer.

The timeline on the left hand side (Source B) comes from a book called *The Crusades Through Arab Eyes* by Amin Maalouf, a writer from Lebanon. This book was written in 1983.

The timeline on the right hand side (Source C) comes from a British writer of children's books. It was written in 1975.

Look at both lists very carefully and try to find some similarities and differences between them. To make it easier, we have chosen only a few dates from the original timelines.

B A timeline from *The Crusades through Arab Eyes* by Amin Maalouf, 1983.

Before Invasion

622 the emigration – or hijra – of the Prophet Muhammad from Makkah to Madinah. Beginning of the Muslim calendar.

1071 the Seljuk Turks crush the Byzantines at Malazgend [Manzikert] and seize Asia Minor [Turkey]. They soon control the entire Muslim East except for Egypt.

Invasion 1096–1100

1096 Kilij Arslan, Sultan [ruler] of Nicea, crushes a Frankish invasion army led by Peter the Hermit.

1097 first great Frankish expedition. Nicea is taken; Kilij Arslan is defeated at Dorylaeum.

1098 the [Western Europeans] take Edessa and then Antioch, and victory over a Muslim rescue army . . . The incident of cannibalism in Ma'arra.

1099 fall of Jerusalem, followed by death and destruction. Failure of the Egyptian rescue army . . . Al-Harawi leads a group of refugees to Baghdad to complain about the lack of action by Muslim leaders.

Occupation 1100–1128

1108 strange battle near Tel Bashir – two armies of Islamic and Frankish soldiers fight each other.

Pushed back 1128–1146

1144 Zangi takes Edessa, destroying the first of the four Frankish states of the East.

Victory 1146–1187

1148 failure at Damascus for a new Frankish expedition led by Conrad, Emperor of Germany, and Louis VII, King of France.

1171 Saladin . . . sole master of Egypt.

1187 The Year of Victory

Saladin crushes the Frankish armies at Hattin, near Lake Tiberias. He reconquers Jerusalem and the greater part of the Frankish territories. The occupiers now hold only Tyre, Tripoli and Antioch.

Reprieve [relief from trouble] 1187–1244

1190–92 setback for Saladin at Acre. Richard the Lionheart, King of England, enables the Franj [Western Europeans] to recover several cities from the sultan, but not Jerusalem.

C A timeline from *Knights and Crusades* by Michael Gibson, written in 1975.

Events Leading Up to the Crusades

632 death of Muhammad.
1071 the Seljuk Turks defeat the Byzantines.
1076 the Turks capture Jerusalem. They treat the Christian pilgrims very carefully.

First Crusade 1096–1099

1099/15 July crusaders capture Jerusalem.
22 July Godfrey de Bouillon is elected king – the crusading states are set up.

Second Crusade 1147–1149

1144 a Turkish leader called Zangi attacks and captures the town of Edessa. Louis VII of France and Conrad III of Germany set off for the Holy Land.
1148 the crusaders besiege Damascus unsuccessfully. The crusade is a failure.

Third Crusade 1189–1192

1187 Saladin, Sultan of Egypt, defeats Guy of Jerusalem at the Battle of Hattin.
1190 Richard I of England and Philip Augustus of France sail for Palestine.
1191 Siege of Acre. The crusaders win.
1191 Battle of Arsuf. Richard I defeats Saladin.
1191 truce between Richard I and Saladin. Christians are allowed to visit Jerusalem.

1 a) Write a list of three differences between the two timelines.
b) Write a list of three things that both timelines mention.
c) Try to explain *why* the timelines are so different.
d) Now compare source B with the timeline at the front of the book.
  i) What differences do you notice?
  ii) Why are they different?

2 a) Sources B and C are different. Does this mean that one is right and the other wrong? Explain your answer.
b) Using the rest of the book and these two timelines make up your own timeline of the crusades. *But* you can only have a maximum of 10 dates in it with as many sub-headings as you like.
c) Compare your timeline with those of other people in your class and talk about the similarities and differences in them.

3 Look at source D.
a) Describe what you can see in the picture.
b) How does source D help you answer the question: 'How did the crusaders fight battles?'

D The Battle of Dorylaeum 1097. The crusaders defeated the Turks. It was an important victory for the crusaders.

Crusading didn't suddenly stop in 1291. Were the crusades just a series of invasions to take land in the Middle East? In this unit we want you to think about why western countries have been involved in the affairs of the Middle East for centuries.

Below are just a few examples of western countries and their interests in the Middle East.

Napoleon in Egypt 1798

The French general Napoleon Bonaparte invaded the Middle East in 1798. He defeated the Mamluk rulers of Egypt at the Battle of the Pyramids and attacked Syria. His aim was to threaten British trade with the East and India.

The British Royal Navy managed to destroy most of the French ships which had brought Napoleon's forces there and to supply the Turkish forces fighting the French. Napoleon was forced to return to Europe in 1799. He had taken with him a number of scientists who began to make some important discoveries about the history of Egypt.

The First World War 1914-18

The Ottoman Turks were on Germany's side in the First World War and so the British and French tried to defeat them. General Allenby was largely responsible for the allied victory after defeating the Turks in Palestine and Syria.

It had been a hard fight and promises were made to local Arab and Jewish people in order to gain their support.

Mandates 1919

In 1919, after the end of the First World War in 1918, land which had once belonged to the defeated Turks was put under the control of Britain and France. It was hoped that the areas, or *mandates* as they were called, would one day become independent. Britain took charge of Palestine and Iraq. France took charge of Syria and the Lebanon. Both countries were keen to control these important areas because of their trading and military value.

A Painting of the Battle of the Pyramids, 1798.

B In 1991 the USA and several European countries took part in a war to free Kuwait – and the large oilfields there – from the control of her neighbour, Iraq.

Over a period of time some things change. Some things do not. When things do not change we call this continuity.

C An American oil company executive remembers how little his friends knew about Islam. From *Kings and Camels* by Grant Butler, quoted in *Approaches to Islam* by Richard Tames (1982).

During our first week at the Aramco School on Long Island, questions were asked of us to find out our general knowledge of the Arab world.

One of our members thought that Islam was a 'game of chance, similar to bridge'. Another said it was a 'mysterious sect founded in the south by the Ku Klux Klan'. The Prophet Muhammad was thought to be the man who 'wrote the Arabian Nights'. One of the more reasonable answers came from one of our men who said 'Muhammad had something to do with a mountain. He either went to the mountain or it came to him.'

1 Using the evidence in this unit, copy and complete the chart to show western involvement in the Middle East.

People	Date	Event	Reason

2 a) From this unit make a list of the reasons why European countries got involved in the affairs of the Middle East. (Include this in the fourth column of the chart above.)
b) 'European countries have always wanted to take over land in the Middle East.' Do you agree with this sentence? Explain your answer carefully.

3 Using your school library find out as much as you can about the following events. Add them to your chart:
a) Battle of Lepanto 1571.
b) Rommel in Egypt 1942.
c) Suez Crisis 1956.

4 There are different ways of looking at the crusades, for example: (i) The crusades were religious pilgrimages, or (ii) the crusades were military invasions. Which of these two ideas seems better to fit the evidence? Explain your answer and look back through the book to find examples.

GLOSSARY

asses – donkeys

astrolabe – device for measuring the position of stars

astronomers – people who study the stars and planets

balustrade – row of pillars supporting a rail

canon – an official of the Christian Church, usually working in a cathedral

chaplains – officials in the Christian Church

Christian – a follower of Jesus Christ

Chronicle – a record of events

civilisations – people with laws, education, government and the arts

clerics – minor officials of the Christian Church

clip – to cut a piece from something – in this case a coin

dethrone – to remove from the throne

devout – believes in something a great deal

dismembering – cutting or breaking into pieces

emir – an Islamic official

enslaved – was made a slave

epileptic – a person with a disorder of the nervous system

faith – strong belief in religion

feudal system – a way of organising people and work – used to describe the Middle Ages

Franks – used to describe most people from West Europe in the Middle Ages

hermit – a person living completely alone

irrigation – man-made watering system for the land

Islam – the Muslim religion

Jews – people of Hebrew origins, whose religion is Judaism

keep – the stone stronghold of a castle

Makkah – a holy place of Islam, in present-day Saudi Arabia

manuscript – a written document

martyrs – people who die for their religious belief

medieval – of the Middle Ages

Mihrab – niche in the wall of a mosque which faces the holy city of Makkah

military orders – Christian religious fighting groups

minarets – tall slender towers on mosques, from which the followers of Islam are called to prayer

Muslims – believers in Islam

Mongols – central Asian people

navigators – people who find the correct direction to travel in

novel – story book

oath – a promise to do something

orphan – someone whose parents are dead

paradise – a land of plenty, with no work

peasants – poor farm workers

pilgrimage – a journey to a holy place

pilgrims – travellers on special journeys to holy places

pillage/plunder – to steal and destroy

Pope – leader of the Catholic Church

principality – land belonging to a prince

prophets – people who are believed to speak God's words

quarters – the place where people live

ransom – money demanded to return a kidnapped person

refugees – people forced out of their homes

retainers – followers of a wealthy person

sacrifice – give up something for a good cause

Saracens – name for Muslims and Arabs at the time of the crusades

scalping – removing the skin and hair from the skull

scholars – people studying something

sect – a group of people who all believe in something

siege – the attack on a town, city or castle

siege engines – machines used during a siege

spire – pointed tower on a church

stature – size

tactless – rude and thoughtless

treaties – agreements between governments

truce – agreement to stop fighting

tyrant – a strong and unpleasant ruler

unbelievers – people who don't believe in a certain religion

vintner – wine maker

vizier – important Islamic official

vow – promise to do something